The gunmakers of Lincolnshire and its environs

Tom Wimsey
(1937–97)

Edited and with contributions by
Arthur G. Credland

Basiliscoe Press   MONOGRAPH NO 2

This publication has been made possible by a contribution from the A.V.B. Norman Research Trust.

Front cover: Lithograph, 1847 by T. W. Wallis, of Upgate, Louth; Mr Dodson standing outside his shop at number 14 and a pair of percussion pistols signed LIVERSIDGE GAINSBRO on the tang behind the hammer (Hull Museum)

Back cover: Upper; Receipted bill 12 November 1789, Durs Egg to Sir John Nelthorpe Bart.(Lincolnshire Archives NEL 9/11/51). Lower; Bill from William Bishop to Sir John Nelthorpe 1836, settled 1844 (Lincolnshire Archives NEL 8/1/30).

© Tom Wimsey and Arthur G. Credland, 2011

ISBN 978-0-9551622-3-7

Published by
Basiliscoe Press
Hawthorne Cottage
Moorfield Road
Leeds
LS12 3SE
UK

Design by Dazeye

Printed and bound by Henry Ling Limited, Dorchester

Contents

Preface	5
Introduction	8
Gunmakers, by town:	
Grantham	**15**
Newton	15
Wilkins	19
Dawson (and Stamford)	20
Lincoln	**22**
Claborough	22
Hanson	25
Wallis	27
Louth	**30**
Gunnis	30
Chapman	31
Tate	32
Lill	34
Kew	39
Dodson	40
West (and Retford)	44
Godsall	50
Lingard (and Grimsby)	51
Hodgson	52

Contents

Stamford   57
Edson   57
Monck   58

Annotated Directory;   61
including Loughborough and Melton Mowbray (Leics.), Wisbech (Cambridgeshire), Nottingham, Newark (Notts.)

Acknowledgements   85
Appendix: The Nelthorpe archive   86
Notes   91

Preface

The main centres of gunmaking in Lincolnshire were Grantham, Louth and Lincoln, which are described in some detail. Especial notice is made of Louth a thriving and populous market town with more than 600 inhabitants and a market at the time of Domesday. It is the focal point of north-east Lincolnshire and is situated east of Lincoln on the main road between Boston and Sleaford in the south and Grimsby (on the Humber) in the north. Boston was a not insignificant port through many centuries and remains so down to the present; it is linked southwards through Spalding to Stamford and the Great North Road.

The Newtons of Grantham have been dealt with previously (see note 1) but this nursery of gunmakers demands more detailed treatment at some future date. The town provided London with a number of fine gunsmiths and there were long established links between Grantham and the capital. It is interesting to note that the bride of Joseph Heylin, gunmaker (married 25 November 1759 at Cornhill) was one Anne Greenhaugh, spinster of the parish of Grantham, 'of the age of thirty years and upwards'. (Norman Dixon, 'Joseph Heylin a Georgian gunmaker, 1780–1801', *Journal of the Arms and Armour Society*, vol. XVII No.7, March 2002, p.162)

The main routes crossing Lincolnshire create links across county boundaries and some brief notice is made of Melton Mowbray (Leicestershire) on the road between Gainsborough and Leicester and also Wisbech (Cambridgeshire) south of Boston and on the way to Kings Lynn and Norwich.

George West of Louth moved away from what was once a hive of gunsmiths to Retford in Nottinghamshire, a little way south west of Gainsborough, not only situated on the Great North Road but amidst the great estates of the 'Dukeries'.

Brigg, a once thriving farming community, has a number of adjoining estates including Elsham and Scawby–the home of the Nelthorpes. It is

TThe late Tom Wimsey (1937-97) holding the double-barrelled 8 bore fowling piece, signed WEST on the lock plate and LOUTH on the spine.

also only a short distance south of Barton-on-Humber, once the major landing place for Humber ferries and formerly a port with old established links to the continent, especially the Netherlands.

Lincoln is centrally placed in Lincolnshire on the high road (the Roman Ermine Street) between Sleaford and Peterborough to the south and Barton-on-Humber to the north.

Stamford with its key position on the Great North Road attracted gunsmiths from nearby Grantham some of whom still maintained a presence in that town. Similarly in Yorkshire, but from an earlier generation, it is no coincidence that Henry Ellis (d. 1722/3) active as a gunmaker from about 1690 to 1712, a maker of high quality firearms, was situated on the Great North Road, at Doncaster, a magnet for the horse-racing gentleman long before the institution of the St Leger.

Grantham, Stamford and Boston are the key towns in the southern half of Lincolnshire but at the time of the 1841 census the most populous towns were Horncastle, with a population of around 10,000 including surrounding districts, and Louth with nearly 9000 residents. Gainsborough had some 7000 people, more than double the count for Lincoln. Boston had a population of some 3500, Alford about 2000 and Brigg slightly less than 2000. In the second half of the century the focus shifts decidedly towards Lincoln which grows as a centre of engineering and the metal fabrication trades. Dominated by great companies such as Rustons it was where the first tanks were developed during the 1914–18 war. Grimsby also grew apace after the arrival of the railway in 1848, which stimulated the growth of the fishing industry but the market towns have declined in the twentieth century. Urban Grimsby however never attracted a significant gunmaking trade, which increasingly became concentrated in Lincoln, a centre for engineering in the modern era but set in a rural landscape.

The text which follows reproduces all of Tom Wimsey's notes carefully gleaned over fifteen or more years with some updates where appropriate.

Arthur G. Credland

Introduction
Birmingham, London and the gun trade

Early firearms were made by blacksmiths and the accompanying stock by a carpenter. The crude handguns of the 14th and 15th centuries were utilitarian weapons made for the field of battle. Ignition was achieved by dipping a lighted slow match into the priming powder which in turn set off the main charge. Such weapons could not easily be used on horseback and were not very convenient for hunting. They therefore generally lacked status and were not regularly given a superior finish or highly decorated.

The invention of the wheellock in the early 16th century provided a means of self-ignition by which pressure on the trigger released a serrated wheel to rub against a piece of pyrites. The resulting shower of sparks inflamed the priming powder. Pistols and carbines with such a mechanism could be deployed on horseback; they became an important cavalry arm in the 17th century and a weapon appropriate for a gentleman. The wheellock was also useful for the hunting field and the gun could be held cocked and ready to fire while lying in wait for the prey. These were interesting mechanical devices and princes and titled gentlemen commissioned expensive and often elaborately decorated examples as hunting weapons or as cabinet pieces to show off to their contemporaries.

In England London was the centre of production of firearms since the proximity of court and parliament and the presence of wealthy merchants provided a concentration of clients which encouraged craftsmen, including gunmakers, to set up their workshops in the capital. Many of these craftsmen relied to a greater or lesser extent on the monarch and the wealthy aristocrats in his orbit.

By the end of the 17th century the flintlock mechanism was universally accepted as the simplest and most effective form of ignition. The jaws of the cock held a piece of flint which, when the trigger was pulled, fell forwards and struck sparks from the steel. A lot of time might be expended on behalf of the wealthier customer producing a finely balanced lock with a smooth action but an efficient version could be made relatively cheaply suitable for workaday civilian arms as well as for military weapons.

In the early 18th century Birmingham became a serious competitor to the London gun-making trade and supplying huge quantities of slave guns for Africa boosted production considerably. Large numbers of components were also sold to London contractors for making up into trade guns for the Hudson Bay Company.

Over many generations a variety of metal workers had become concentrated in the Midlands, where fuel (charcoal and coal), metals and water power were available in abundance, and this pool of skilled workmen was the basis of the expanding gun making trade.

At this time most towns of any size would have a gun maker who would assemble and finish weapons from components largely produced by a variety of specialists in their own workshop or in the neighbourhood. Barrel making was often beyond them but might be supplied by a local manufacturer or brought up from London. A growing reputation and increasing production meant that more and more gunmakers obtained their gun barrels from Birmingham and by this is meant not the city of Birmingham as we know it now but the town, and outlying settlements in Warwickshire (which were eventually absorbed into greater Birmingham) and Staffordshire.

Barrels were forged from an iron strip bent around a mandrel and the seam welded up. Better quality tubes of the late 18th and 19th centuries, Damascus or stub twist, were made by first twisting bundles of iron and steel rods which were hammered flat and the resulting strip wound around the mandrel. The edges were lap welded, followed by boring and polishing and the resulting barrel with a fabric of intermingled iron and steel was tough and elastic, well able to withstand the explosion of the powder charge necessary to propel the lead ball each time weapon was fired.

Barrels were tested or proved by igniting a much larger charge of powder than would be the case in normal usage inserted in the unfinished barrel. If it survived undamaged this extreme charge it would be regarded as safe and the barrel appropriately stamped or marked. There was a proof house in London in 1797 but around the country individual gun barrel makers or gunmakers, like Edward Newton of Grantham, who made their own barrels, also proved them. The Birmingham Proof House was established in 1813 and by the Gun Barrel Proof Act of the same year it was made compulsory for barrels to be proved in either London or Birmingham.

Birmingham increased its production to supply the trade at large with barrels, locks and gun furniture made by a large number of craftsmen working by themselves or in small groups in independent workshops. Each man had his bench, anvil, a vice, and a set of hand tools and worked at piece-work rates on the particular component he specialised in and according to the pattern provided by the contractor. A gun maker would then buy locks, stocks and barrels to assemble in his own workshop and put his signature to the finished product. The demands of the military encouraged mechanisation and after the middle of the 19th century milling (shaping) machines began to be used for lock parts, as well as for cutting stocks, and boring and polishing barrels. Barrel makers were the first members of the trade to introduce water power, early in the 19th century, and water and later steam power provided the motive power linked to series of belts which drove the various machines. The inevitable consequence was the eventual application of the factory system to the gun trade and large numbers of steam hammers, stamps and drills were brought together under one roof.

Both London and the provincial gun makers were finding it more economical to purchase either completed firearms or parts from Birmingham makers. Production of components elsewhere in the provinces diminished rapidly after the middle of the 18th century.

Even without mechanisation and factory-based mass production huge quantities of components had been made in the Midlands, supplied by the hundreds of outworkers. In the period of the Napoleonic wars, 1804–15, a total of 7,660,229 complete arms and parts were produced and in addition nearly a million more components were made for setting up in London as well as some half million sporting arms.

In the 1820s the percussion lock was perfected, following the experiments of the Reverend Alexander Forsyth in Scotland, and this provided reliable ignition in wet and windy conditions which for the flintlock could result in the priming powder being lost or dampened with resulting misfires. A copper cap, placed on top of a nipple, contained a small amount of fulminating powder and when struck by the hammer, released by pressure on the trigger, sends a flame straight through to the main charge in the barrel. The gun trade took this new development in its stride and as the century progressed production of flintlocks declined and percussion locks were accepted by all but the most conservative of sportsmen. Large amounts of flintlock weapons however were still sold for trading in Africa and elsewhere in the Empire. From the outset of the percussion era provincial 'gun makers' were putting their name to a product that had less and less input from themselves or their assistants, most were now retailers rather than makers. The increasing quantity post-1800 of look-alike pistols and long guns, by an ever-growing number of gun makers in the capital and throughout the country, clearly demonstrate how reliant on the Birmingham gun trade were both the London and provincial makers.

The establishment of the new government factory at Enfield, in 1855, to make military arms was inimical to the handmade manufacture in Birmingham while the American Civil War though initially boosting business led eventually to the development of a strong independent gun trade in the USA. After the middle of the 19th century the new breech loading weapons and the requirements of the military for greater quality control and standardisation in manufacture to ensure interchangeability of parts made the extension of the factory system inevitable. Only the part of the trade providing high quality sporting and luxury weapons enabled the survival of some of these specialist outworkers and a few gunmakers workshops with dedicated teams of craftsmen. Even today a handful of true gun makers survive, makers of shot guns and sporting rifles such as Holland & Holland and Purdey, supplying 'best' guns, tailor-made for each individual customer.

Provincial gun making

In general we can say that gun making in Lincolnshire and the location of these craftsmen is much like that in any other county except that the number of large towns compared with the overall size of the county are few and far between; Lincoln, Grimsby and Scunthorpe being the only major centres of population other than the market towns. These urban centres with growing populations and at the same time serving a large rural community provided the right conditions for specialist craftsmen such as gun makers to thrive. Large engineering enterprises which blossomed in the 19th century transformed the quiet cathedral town of Lincoln, while the development of the docks and fishing industry encouraged the expansion of Grimsby and steelmaking had a similar effect on Scunthorpe.

A broad clientele was available to market towns like Grantham located on the Great North Road with a good passing trade as well as the surrounding rural community. Surviving weapons show the high quality of firearms made by the Newton family and wealthy clients such as the Duke of Atholl probably dropped in at the shop while travelling between Scotland and London, or sought it out as a result of the recommendation of someone who had discovered this remarkable workshop while following this great highway.

The skills of the Newton family were handed on to members of another generation who were to make their reputation in the metropolis, notably Twigg, Wogdon and Manton. Apprenticed to Edward Newton, John Fox Twigg and Robert Wogdon received their freedom on the same day, 18 February 1756. Twigg's guns and pistols were some of the finest examples of their kind in the 18th century. The patronage of the Duke of Atholl passed from Newton to Twigg and a pistol described by Neal and Back is fitted with a barrel signed by his former master. This, still in its original chamois leather purse, was found a number of years ago in the padding of the left shoulder of an antique coat at a tailors in Savile Row. Durs Egg, another of the very finest gun makers of the 18th century, worked with Twigg before setting up on his own.

John Manton (1752–1834) was made free in 1775 after completing his time with William and John Ed(g)son jointly, though he had originally been apprenticed to John Dixon of Leicester in 1766. John Edson had himself only completed his apprenticeship with his father William in 1773. No actual retail shop has been located for the Edsons and it has been suggested that William may have been foreman of Newton's establishment. After moving to London, as a foreman to John Fox Twigg, Manton set up on his own account at 6 Dover Street, was subsequently appointed 'gunmaker in ordinary' to George IV and died three years later. His brother Joseph (Joe) Manton was apprenticed to him and they were two of the outstanding gun makers of the period, producing a great variety of firearms of the highest quality.

Wogdon was the most celebrated maker of duelling pistols of his day and it was he and Twigg who defined the weapon as a distinct type. The Mantons brought the duelling pistol to the peak of its development and cased examples with a full set of accessories are nowadays much sought after by collectors. It may be noted that Sir John Nelthorpe Bart (1745–99) of Scawby, Lincolnshire, patronised the young John Manton as early as 1782 at his Dover Street shop which had been opened only since the previous autumn.

The earliest Lincolnshire gunmaker of which we have a record is William Gunnis, active in the mid to late 17th century who is known to have worked as a whitesmith for Louth Corporation. Unfortunately no details of his career or examples of his work have been discovered. Chapman of Louth was active as a gun barrel maker in the late 18th century evidenced by a gun signed Monck of Stamford on the lock and attributed to Thomas Monck. Chapman may also have been a gunmaker while Edward Newton was not only a gun maker but made barrels which he supplied to other makers too. Henry Godsall, probably the son of Henry

Godsall of Gloucester, was a gun barrel maker who retired to Louth after a career in London, during which he served eight years in the workshop of Joseph Manton. In the 19th century much of the gun making talent seems to have resided in Louth but no direct tradition can be traced back into earlier times to link such men as Bryan and Richard Tate with William Gunnis some two hundred years before.

Though of Lincolnshire origin Samuel Newton, based himself in Nottingham no doubt to distance himself from his brother Edward and establish an independent business beyond the environs of Grantham. The Newtons represent the peak of true gun making in the county with each weapon being very much a product of their own workshop, often including the barrel. Thereafter the firearms from Grantham and the rest of the county were increasingly built from Birmingham parts and after about 1830–40 most of the items retailed here, as elsewhere, had been made up in Birmingham and just signed with the local man's name.

In the 19th century gun makers are often incomers from outside the county, some migrating from the Birmingham trade, others from adjacent counties. Cartmell of Lincoln was the son of Thomas Cartmell of Doncaster and John Hanson of Lincoln was almost certainly related to George and Nathan Hanson, also of Doncaster. Gunmaking in the south Yorkshire town can be traced back to the 17th century and like Grantham and Stamford in Lincolnshire Doncaster is on the route of the Great North Road.

Arthur G. Credland

Further reading
Bailey, de Witt & D A Nie 1978 *English gunmakers: the Birmingham and provincial gun trade in the 18th and 19th* centuries. Arms and Armour Press, London.
Blair, C 1962 *European and American arms*. Batsford, London.
Neal, W K 1975 *Great British Gunmakers 1740–1790: the history of John Twigg and the Packington* guns. Sotheby, Parke Bernet, London.

Gunmakers–biographies

Grantham

The Newtons are the key gunmaking family in Grantham and their workshop was the nursery for some of the finest gunmakers of the 18th century. The following is a summary based on Tom Wimsey's detailed description published by the Arms and Armour Society in 2000.

Edward Newton (c. 1692–1764)

Edward Newton was born, probably in 1692, the son of Samuel Newton and Elizabeth St(r)elley living at South Wingfield, Derbyshire. Received as a 'foreigner' in 1718 he compounded with a fee to admit him to the freedom of his craft as gunsmith in Grantham. Already 26 years old he would be some five years out of his apprenticeship but it is not known to whom he was indentured and where he had worked as a journeyman in the meantime. Edward's brother Samuel was also a gunsmith, in Nottingham , where he remained till at least 1764.

In 1719 Edward settled in premises on the east side of Market Place (figure 2), his shop facing the Great North Road and the Angel, a notable coaching inn, just four doors away. Five years later he had moved to the other side of Market Place almost opposite the Angel inn. Two of his apprentices, Cornelius Lenton and William Simpson, were granted their freedom in 1733. The latter is probably the Simpson of Castlegate, York, c.1738–56, responsible for the highly decorated fowling piece, now in the Royal Armouries. Made in 1738, or shortly before, it is said to have belonged to William Constable of Burton

figure 2: Edward Newton's premises, east side of Market Place (High street), fronting the Great North road, occupied c.1719-26. Demolished 1910; large three storey building on the left is the Exchange Hall, built 1852.

Constable, East Yorkshire. Valued at 50 guineas it was raffled by the maker at a guinea a ticket (*York Courant* 11 July 1738; I am indebted to Dr. David Connell, Director of the Burton Constable Foundation for bringing this reference to my attention; editor). Illustrated is a gun, 52¾ inches long overall, which was part of the gun cabinet of the Whig grandee Charles Watson Wentworth, 2nd Marquess of Rockingham (1730-82) of Wentworth Woodhouse. The rear, octagonal, portion of the barrel, 38 inches long, is struck with a crowned P (for private proof) the initials EN and a four petalled rose. The choice of a rose may have been influenced by the presence of the Rose tavern nearby–a stone tablet with the date 1606 and a Tudor rose (but five petalled) can still be seen let into the gable wall of a building where the tavern once stood.

The top flat of the barrel is inscribed E. NEWTON GRANTHAM. There is a silver foresight and a stud on the underside of the muzzle for receiving a hunting bayonet. A compartment in the butt for the bayonet, now missing, has a hinged metal cover engraved 6, the number of the weapon in the gun cabinet. A most unusual feature is the pivoted steel which can be swung out making the gun completely safe and impossible to shoot (figures 3 and 4).

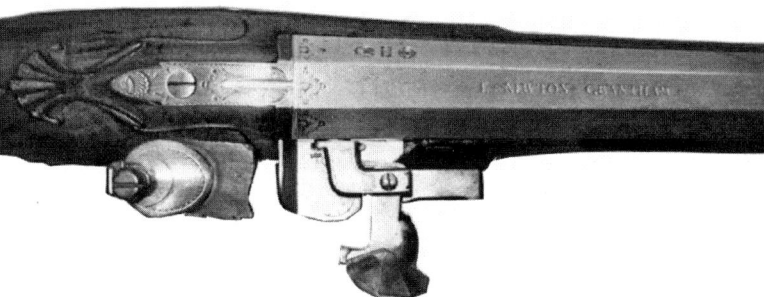

Above: figure 3: Detail of the Rockingham gun, inscribed E.NEWTON GRANTHAM. The steel is swung outwards in the safe position.

Right: figure 4: Breech of Rockingham gun, c.1750, showing barrel stamps (formerly in the collection of the late A.N.Kennard).

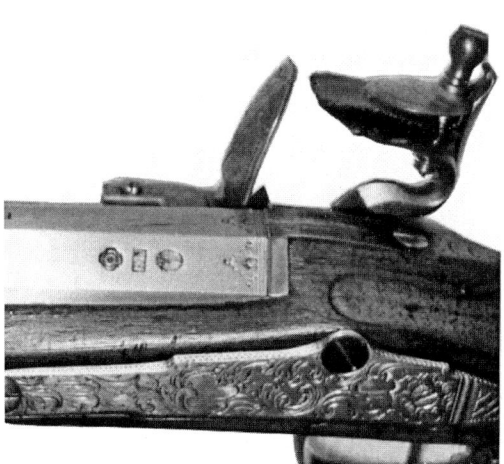

Typical of the period Newton was also a gun barrel maker and the monogram EN can be observed both on weapons made by himself and barrels supplied to other makers. In 1739 Newton married Mrs Catherine Bacon, a widow, and in 1748 Robert Wogdon commenced his seven year apprenticeship with Newton. Wogdon is one of the best known names in British gunmaking and is regarded as a maker of the finest quality duelling pistols. Wogdon and John Twigg each received their freedom in 1756; the latter was probably also an apprentice of Newton's and he also established an eminent reputation in London.

Edward Newton's clients included the Duke of Atholl and the 2nd Marquess of Rockingham who no doubt dropped into his workshop when travelling the Great North Road between their respective homes and London; they may well have stayed at the Angel Inn. Newton died in May 1764 and was buried in St Wulframs churchyard, Grantham, leaving his stock-in-trade, goods and utensils to his nephew, William Newton, who continued in the Market Place premises.

It is worth noting here the 14 bore flintlock gun of about 1755 by Edward Newton of Grantham which was sold from the W Keith Neal collection as lot 57. It was made for Evelyn Pierrepoint (1711–73) 2nd Duke of Kingston upon Hull, who lived at Thoresby Park, Notts. In the same sale, lot 206, was a 54 bore flintlock pistol by John Twigg with a barrel made by Edward Newton who was probably his master. A pair of side lock cannon-barrelled holster pistols, silver mounted, c. 1770, signed E Newton converted to percussion were sold as lot 1237 in the sale of the arms and armour collection of John Bourne at John Taylors auction room, Louth, on the 22 July 1981.

A Queen Anne pistol signed Newton of Grantham, with walnut butt and silver grotesque mask, hall-marked 1780, was offered for sale by Garth Vincent Antiques in 2004. It has an 8 inch cannon barrel, silver dragon side plate, silver escutcheon and silver wire inlay in the butt behind the breech. Illustrated in the January/February *Classic Arms and Militaria*, no. 1, p.42 is a magnificent pair of 18 bore flint lock pistols with Birmingham hallmarks for 1775. Each of the blued swamped, two-stage barrels are engraved Grantham and struck with the maker's mark of William Newton on the octagonal breech. Full walnut stocks with silver foresights, pommels and escutcheons each engraved with the Riddle crest and the motto 'The right to share'; the ram rods are ivory tipped and the lid of the mahogany case is engraved C.B. Riddle Esq. In the Preston Hall Museum, Stockton-on-Tees is a brass eprouvette (inv. no. SB73) with brass wheel, marked 1 to 8, 6 in overall, signed NEWTON near muzzle of barrel (figures 5 and 6).

figures 5 (above) & 6 (below): Brass eprouvette signed NEWTON; Preston Hall, Stockton-on-Tees. Left and right sides. of 17 Broad Street, Spalding; photographed in 2003.

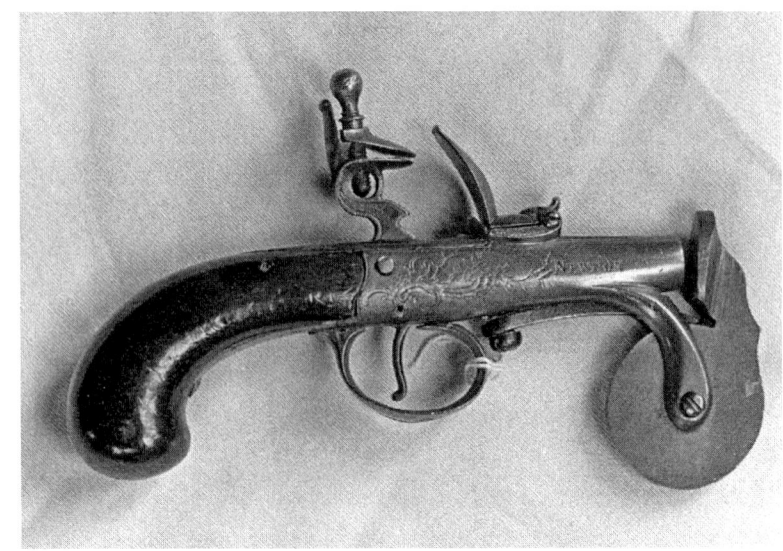

A 12 bore sporting gun was sold at Bonhams as lot 19 of 'Fine Antique Firearms from the W. Keith Neal Collection' (10 November 2005) signed E. Newton Grantham on a rectangular plate let into the breech of a three stage barrel (42⅛ inches) which also bears Newton's own barrel mark. Made for Alexander 10th Earl of Eglinton (1723–69; friend and benefactor of James Boswell, he was murdered by a trespasser on his estate) the silver side plate is in the form of a pike and the escutcheon a cock pheasant perched up a tree, with the London hallmark and the initials JA, probably of Jeconiah Ashley. It has a gold-lined touch hole, rounded lock signed on a baldachin surmounted by a scallop shell, a sliding safety catch behind the cock, the latter with foliate details chiselled in relief on the upper jaw and screw. The full stock of figured walnut is carved in relief with overlapping shells behind the barrel tang. This weapon was sold as lot 335 in Bonhams sale of 'Fine antique arms and armour' 29 April 2010.

Corrigenda

To 'Newton of Grantham' *Journal of the Arms and Armour Society* vol.xvi, no.5, September 2000: p.279, note 9, for page 191 read p.155; on page 281, note 38, add 'At the same court William Edson (see below) purchased his freedom'; p.291, pl.6 for Sir Brownlow Cusk read Sir Brownlow Cust.

William Newton (1722-90)

Born in Nottingham the son of Samuel Newton, gun maker, he was as a 'foreigner' admitted to the freedom of Grantham on payment of a fee of £20. This was on 17 May only days after his uncle's death. John Newton, son of Edward's brother Philip, was already in the workshop and was granted his freedom in 1765, subsequently entering employment with John Twigg. There are few details available of Newton's clientele but we do know that Sir Brownlow Cust of Belton Hall was a customer.

Thomas Monck was apprenticed to William, granted his freedom in 1771 and set up in business in Red Lion square, Stamford, some twenty miles away and also on the Great North Road. Another apprentice, Edward Fisher, was granted his freedom in 1775.

In 1765, soon after William Newton came to Grantham, William Edson, a 'foreigner', was admitted a freeman on payment of £20 and became a direct competitor of the Newton shop. John Manton (see below–under Thomas Manton, Stamford), who became one of the great names in the London trade was jointly apprenticed to William and John Edson and granted his freedom in 1775.

John Wilkins, admitted to his freedom in 1783 was almost certainly apprenticed to William Newton. Certainly he was employed in the workshop, was a witness to Newton's will and on the latter's death 23 October 1790, aged 68, Wilkins took over the business. Like his uncle Newton was buried in St Wulframs churchyard and after a span of more than 72 years the name of Newton, gun maker, disappeared from the town of Grantham.

John Wilkins and John William Burton Wilkins, gunpowder suppliers

A newspaper cutting dated 2 August 1839 has the following:

> To Sportsmen. I.W.B. Wilkins, Grantham, continues to supply consumers of gunpowder with that article of every quality, manufactured by either Messrs. Pigou and Wilks of Dartford, Curtis and Harvey of Hounslow and Lawrence and Son, Battle, at the same price those firms

charge all dealers and retailers and consequently at considerably less cost than any consumer would procure it, even from the manufacturers themselves.

Per cask of 100lbs

Best treble strong, in canisters	£12.0 or 2s. 6d per lb.
Best treble strong, in paper	£10.15 or 2s. 3d.
Best double strong, D.D.S in paper	£9.10 or 2s. 0d.
Double strong, second quality, D.S	£8.10 or 1s. 10d.
Third quality	£4.10 or 1s. 0d.

Orders for casks containing 25, 50 or 100 lbs., forwarded direct from the mills.

N.B. Patent shot, percussion caps, etc. Letters to be post paid.

At High Street, Grantham, he is recorded in an 1842 directory described as gunpowder preparer and in his full name of John William Burton Wilkins. He was no doubt the son of John Wilkins, partner of William Newton who succeeded to the latter's business in 1790 (Wimsey 2000: 292). Pigots directory for 1819-20 lists 'I Wilkins (the only preparer of the glass gunpowder patronized by HRH the Duke of York), opposite the Angel Inn.'

George Dawson of Grantham and Stamford

Dawson had shops both in Grantham (c. 1834–63) and Stamford. An advertisement in the *Lincoln, Rutland and Stamford Mercury* 24 August, 1838 tells us that:

Mr G Dawson, gun-maker, High Street, Stamford (late with Purday (sic), Oxford Street, London) grateful for the extensive patronage already conferred by the nobility, gentry and sportsmen in general of Stamford, Grantham and their neighbourhoods begs to inform them that he has manufactured for the approaching season a large stock of guns. G.D. calls particular attention to his best guns which for inspection will be found to be made in a superior style, his having had experience in one of the first houses of the present day in London enabling him to make and finish in the neatest possible manner.

G.D. has on sale a variety of second-hand double and single guns–a double Manton, new last year, and scarcely used, which cost £44; and several others of different makes, which will be sold cheap.

A fresh stock of ammunition, etc for the approaching season has been received.

G.D. informs his friends of Grantham and its neighbourhood that he attends there every Saturday at his old shop. Agent Mr. Smith .

A 30 bore percussion target pistol has been recorded, 15 inches long overall with a browned twist, deeply rifled barrel of 9 inches engraved Grantham. Half-stocked, lock engraved Dawson, scroll engraved trigger guard with capstan screw set trigger, brass tipped ebony ramrod and chequered grip , an oval escutcheon with initials WM , offered for sale by Wallis and Wallis 31 October/1 November,1977, sale no 234, lot 783, illustrated pl.37.

Lincoln

Peter Clabrough fl. c. 1821–39, and his successors

Clabrough was active in Lincoln from c. 1821. An advertisement in the *Lincoln, Rutland and Stamford Mercury*, 2 December 1825 (repeated 9 December) brings attention to his stock:

> P. Clabrough, gun-maker, High Street, nearly opposite Butchery Lane, Lincoln, in returning his warmest and most grateful acknowledgements to his numerous friends for the distinguished patronage he has experienced since his establishment in the above business in Lincoln most respectfully takes the present opportunity of informing the nobility, gentlemen and others the sportsmen of the city and neighbourhood, that, from his always having an extensive assortment of guns made in the first style, and on the best improved percussion principles, he hopes, by a strict and unremitting attention to the execution of the orders he may be honoured with, to ensure and merit a continuance of those favours which have been so liberally and kindly conferred upon him and he can with the most perfect confidence recommend and warrant every article from his manufactory to be of the very best materials and workmanship, which he trusts will be found on inspection to be inferior to none in the trade. Gunpowder and shot from the first manufactories.
>
> Joyce and Co.'s * Anti-corrosive Percussion Powder in the form of caps, patches, balls and grain, warranted neither to corrode nor miss fire.
>
> N.B. Trusses of the best quality.

On 7 February of the same year he had advertised for an apprentice. In 1839 Jane Clabrough refers to her deceased husband and she subsequently remarries and becomes Jane Seels, listed as such c. 1848–57. From about 1860 the shop is in the hands of John Hanson and his successors. Hanson

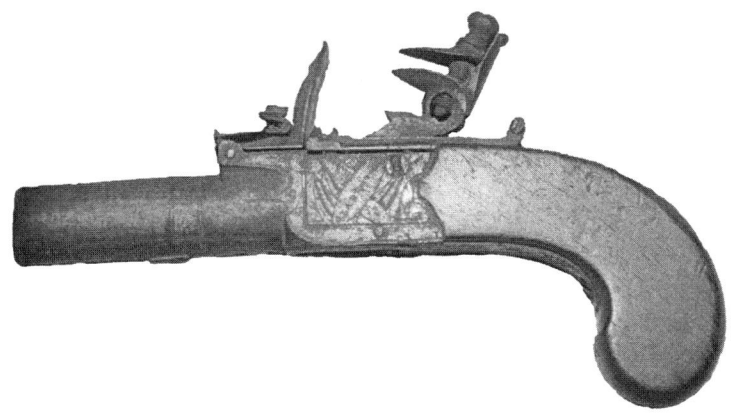

figure 7: Left side view of flintlock, box-lock, pistol signed CLABROUGH, Lincoln (Lincoln County Museum).

is probably the 'superior workman' Jane Clabrough took on in 1846 (see annotated directory below)

A boxlock, flint-lock pistol of typical Birmingham manufacture, signed CLABROUGH and LINCOLN on opposite sides of the lock is preserved in the Lincoln County Museum (figure 7).

Overall length 6¼ inches, barrel 1⅝ inches long and ⁷⁄₁₆ inch bore, furnished with a folding trigger.

A turn-off pocket pistol with folding trigger, of rather better quality is in the Royal Armouries collection (XII 1724). This is a late example of a flintlock pistol, c. 1830, with silver mounts and Birmingham proof marks, CLABROUGH LINCOLN on the barrel; illustrated Claude Blair *European and American Arms*, London 1962 (1964).

John Plumb Clabrough emigrated to the USA and was active in the gun trade in San Francisco from 1862, opening his own shop in 1867. Joined by his brother Joseph in 1870 they returned to England in 1871 setting up a workshop at 5 New Building, Price Street, Birmingham, to supply depots across North America. The name survives in Birmingham until 1937 and it is such an unusual one it is likely that the two brothers were linked to Peter Clabrough. J. P. Clabrough apparently always claimed his birthplace as Yorkshire and an M. Carlton Clabrough was active in Selby as a gun maker in 1857 (Tate 1997: 42–44).

J.P. Clabrough and Bros, were at 8 Whittall Street, Birmingham, in 1880 and later the same year Clabrough Bros. are recorded at 15 St. Mary's Road. In 1888 listed at Whittall Street and St. Mary's Row. From 1895, J.P. Clabrough Brothers and Johnstone, 8 Whittall Street and ditto. Then 7½ St. Mary's Row in 1900 and J.P. Clabrough and Johnstone, 16 and 17 Loveday Street, 1915–30.

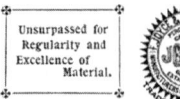

figure 8: Joyces Sporting Cartridges; advertisement in 1895.

Clabrough Bros. were at 52 Leadenhall Street, London c. 1893-95 and Clabrough and Johnstone at 11 Pall Mall c. 1908-14; 143 Holborn, 1915-17; and at 54 Clerkenwell Road c. 1920-31 with a factory in Birmingham. An advertisement in Milward's (of Redditch) price list and catalogue of fishing tackle, c. 1908, claims that the firm was established in 1865.

*The name of Joyce is still to the fore towards the end of the 19th century when 'Joyces Sporting Cartridges' were being sold by F. Joyce and Co. Ltd of 57 Upper Thames Street, London. (figure 8)

W. Cartmell fl. 1825-26

An informative advertisement appears in the *Lincoln, Rutland and Stamford Mercury* 18 November 1825 and is repeated on 25 November:

> W Cartmell, gun-maker, High Street, St Mary le Wigford, informs the nobility, gentlemen and sportsmen that he has commenced business as above, and being supplied by his father T. Cartmell, gun-maker, Doncaster, with the very best workmen and materials he flatters himself by attention to merit a share of their patronage and support. N.B. a fresh supply of gunpowder every month, also shot and every other article of the very best quality.
>
> W.C. is an appointed agent for Messrs Cartmell and Co. Patent Machine-makers, Doncaster, and has always an assortment of machines for public inspection.

He did not stay very long in Lincoln and in the L.R. & S. Mercury, 26 May 1826:

> W. Cartmell, gun-maker, begs to inform his friends and the public that in consequence of having entered into partnership with his father at Doncaster, he is under the necessity of relinquishing his establishment at Lincoln; and is thus taking leave, he cannot omit expressing his most grateful acknowledgements to those gentlemen who have so liberally honoured him with their favors. N.B. Any persons wishing to take the house and shop may have the fixtures at a fair valuation.

Thomas Cartmell was at High Street, Doncaster, from about 1817 and the firm was styled Thomas Cartmell and Son from 1826. Cartmell senior received a British Patent (no. 5033) on 6 November 1824 for a pill-lock self-priming mechanism, the magazine being located in the head of the hammer. There is every possibility he is the same Thomas Cartmell who was in Manchester at 124 Deansgate c. 1799-1803 (Bailey & Nie 1978).

John Hanson fl. 1862–85 and John R. Hanson fl. 1888–92

John Hanson appears in the Lincolnshire directories from c. 1862 taking on the shop which Peter Clabrough and his widow had occupied. Given the links that were forged between Lincoln and Doncaster, albeit briefly by W. Cartmell (1825–26), it is very likely that John Hanson was connected with George Hanson of 28 Baxter Gate, Doncaster (from c. 1857) and Nathan Wadsworth Hanson of Goose Hill and Baxtergate c. 1837– 56. Possibly George and John were the sons of Nathan. George Hanson and his wife were killed by a gunpowder explosion at the Baxtergate premises 3 January 1880 ending the Hanson connection with Doncaster. A Septimus Hanson was at French Gate, Doncaster 1817–22 and Hanson and Co. at Goose Street in 1833. Charles Hanson is recorded at King Street, Huddersfield, in 1829. His signature appears on an air weapon with external lock and an air reservoir in a metal rifle-type butt covered in pig skin. There are two .400 calibre barrels one with round section the other octagonal, signed 'No.1YORK', each with a tap at the breech for loading ; a third, smooth bore barrel , without a tap and intended for muzzle-loading, is fitted with two pipes for a ramrod, now missing.[4]

In Whites directory for Lincolnshire, 1872, J Hanson, Gun Maker 244 High Street, Lincoln

> Begs to call the attention of sportsmen generally to his newly patented C. F. Breech Loading, Double Gun with direct strikers and indicators, showing when loaded, the simplicity of its action. Its superior shooting qualities and durability have met with the highest approval of all purchasers and sportsmen, who acknowledge it one of the strongest and simplest actions out. Pin and muzzle-loading guns at reduced prices. Pistols and rifles of every description. Ammunition from the best makers. Cartridges loaded with best powder only. Gun cases, cartridge machines, game bags and every sporting requisite.

Hanson's patent, No. 2657 for 26 August 1868, is illustrated in this same advertisement and is described by Baker:

> To open this gun the front portion of the trigger guard has to be pulled forwards. Made as one with the front of the guard is the horizontal portion which slides on two guides on the bottom of the action. This slide has linked to it a short lever hung on an horizontal pivot in the action so that, as the slide is pushed forwards, the top of the lever draws back the sliding bolt in the action. The snap spring is a leaf set vertically behind the standing breech.[5] (figure 9)

figure 9: Lincolnshire directory for 1872; Hanson's patent centre-fire breech-loading shotgun.

Two years later, patent number 353 of 1870, for a bolt action was registered. His evident skill and inventiveness strongly suggests he is the 'superior maker' who has been employed by 'some of the principal gunmakers in London and the country' taken on by Jane Clabrough in 1846.

The entry in the 1885 directory is for the executors of J. Hanson and from c. 1888 the proprietor is John R Hanson (successor to J Hanson)' presumably the latter's son or other near relation. In 1888 he describes himself as 'Maker of every description of Hammer and Hammerless Breech-loading guns, Rook and Rabbit Rifles, Revolvers, Air Guns, Gun Cases, Cartridge and Game Bags, Dog Collars, Whips and Chains, Greyhound and Retriever Slips, Rabbit and Vermin Traps, and every Requisite for the complete Sportsman.' He further advertises second hand guns, repairs, re-stocking, browning etc. 'done on the premises' and 'guns made to order ... every description of ammunition in stock' and agent for Westley Richards, and Cos. patent hammerless BL guns and Deeley-Edge Metford rifles.' He claims he had the largest stock of bicycles and tricycles in the town with machines for hire and all sorts of cycle tools and sundries. The whole of this occupying a complete page of the directory. A half-page the next year, in smaller type, repeats the same information. In Kelly's Lincoln directory of 1896 the guns and accessories on offer are essentially as before but he also proclaims the Hanson safety cycle, holder of most of the records in local cycle races for 1895. The old premises at 244 High Street were the gun shop while the cycle works and show room were at Corporation Street.

The Industries of the Eastern Counties, a gazette published in about 1892 is a major source of information. The entry for 'John R. Hanson, Gun,

Rifle and Ammunition maker, 244 High Street' describes the business as 'having been founded upwards of half a century ago' and it goes on 'the peculiar excellence of all weapons made by Mr Hanson being recognised by sportsmen and others many years ago. The premises occupied by this energetic tradesman are of three stories in height, and though the shop is small, it is in every way well adapted to the business carried on. The stock embraces all kinds of sporting rifles and guns from the ponderous 'eight' and 'twelve' bore to the tiny rook rifle. Revolvers and pistols of all the best English, American and Continental makers are also kept in stock, as well as airguns, walking-stick guns, etc. The manufacture of sporting cartridges constitutes also an important item of this business, a special plant having been laid down by Mr Hanson for the express purpose of filling these in a manner ensuring to each the correct charge. The cartridges filled by Mr Hanson are used by most of the best shots of Lincolnshire and the adjacent counties, and the proprietor prides himself on the production of reliable ammunition at the lowest possible prices for each grade. The rapid spread of the cycle industry has induced Mr Hanson to turn his attention to this branch also, with so great a measure of success that he is turning out machines at the most reasonable prices, and also does a large repairing business. At the rear of the shop are situated the workshops, where a competent staff of reliable workmen is engaged. Mr Hanson is well known in and around the city, and in sporting and industrial circles is much respected'. This description evidently predates the separation of the gun and cycle parts of the business, which is apparent in 1896. A Robert Hanson is indicated at 244 High Street in an 1892 directory, probably John Robert Hanson is intended. From c. 1903–10, L Hanson, gun maker and cycle maker is recorded at 1 Cornhill.

In Yorkshire there were various gun makers by the name of Hanson, active in Doncaster; Septimus, French Gate 1817–23; Sarah, Goose Hill 1823; Nathan, Goose Hill, 1837–55 and Baxter Gate 1856; and George, Baxter Gate, 1857–71.

Wallis Brothers fl. 1888–1922

The principals of this firm may well have been the sons or grandsons of Robert Wallis active in Spalding c.1840–63; he is described as a gun maker, clocksmith and bell hanger at Pinchbeck Street, Spalding, in 1849. R Wallis and Son were at 17 Pinchbeck Street c.1868–72. Seth John Wallis is at the same address c.1876–82 and William R. Wallis at 44 Pinchbeck Street 1888–9. These are probably the Wallis Bros. we later find in Lincoln. From c.1888 there are extensive advertisements for the Wallis Bros., initially at 364 High Street then from c.1896–1900 at 156 High Street (figure 10).

Left: figure 10: Lincolnshire directory for 1888; Wallis Bros., 364 High Street, Lincoln.

Below: figure 11: The Wallis Bros. premises in 2001; corner of Portland Street and High Street, divided into two shops.

The address, 364 High Street (figure 11), Lincoln, is almost opposite the former Midland railway station [6], now a shopping centre, and the men are described in 1888 as:

> Electronic and telephonic engineers, bell-hangers, gas-fitters etc. Guns made to order. All kinds of repairs at moderate charges. Guns restocked, re-browned or made up as new. All kinds of ammunition. Cartridges loaded with the best powder of any maker. Powder, shot, wads and caps, for muzzle-loading guns. Electric, pneumatic, or crank bells and telephones, fixed in any part of the Kingdom.

At 156 High Street, 'opposite the Inland Revenue Office' the Wallis Bros. advertised themselves in 1896 as:

> Gun and cycle manufacturers ... cartridge manufacturers and dealers in all kinds of ammunition. Patent ejectors. Hammerless or hammer guns in stock or made to order. Guns restocked, rebrowned and made up as

new. Electric and telephonic engineers, locksmiths and bell hangers. Dealers in all kinds of electrical apparatus. Cycle agents and dealers in all kinds of cycle accessories; also agents for the self sealing air tube.

A similar advertisement in 1899 gives 1 Cornhill as an additional address and proclaims, 'first inventors of hammerless guns, also of the double gun, both locks worked with one trigger'. Another advertisement in the same directory emphasises the cycle making and retailing part of the business, offering 'an Osmond cycle for £12'; and they were agents for this brand as well as Arabs, Crescents, Gendrons and chainless cycles from £16 16s, 'We also build up Eadie, Chatea Lee, B.S.A., Lloyds and Coopers fittings. Two years guarantee with every fitting'. From 1907 until 1922, the latest date discovered, Wallis Bros. were at St Mary's Street as gun makers and cycle agents.

Louth

Louth is situated on the river Ludd between the Wolds to the north and the marshes to the south. It is 20 miles from Grimsby, 26 from Lincoln, 32 from Barton and Boston, 37 from Gainsborough and 60 miles from Stamford at the southern extremity of the county (see sketch map of Louth for shop locations).

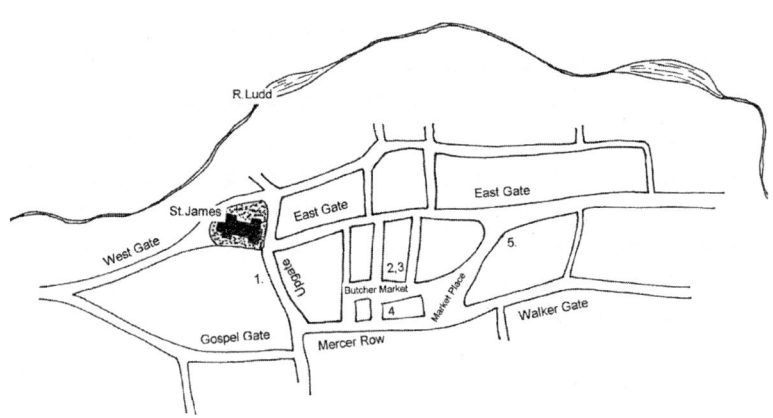

Right: Sketch map of Louth c.1834 showing location of gunsmiths 1. *Upgate* Lill and Dodson; 2, 3. Bryan and Richard Tate; 4. Kew; 5. West.

William Gunnis, 1614–c. 1695

The will of William Gunnis of Louth, dated 1695 proclaims him as a gunsmith.[7] He was born 18 September 1614 at Burgh-le-Marsh, a village some five miles from the Lincolnshire coast on the Skegness to Louth Road. It is not known when he moved to Louth or if he was there during the terrible plague of 1631. No surviving guns are known nor any indication of what range of weapons he produced. The records of Louth Corporation refer only to items usually made by a whitesmith or blacksmith. There is a payment of 6s 2d in 1657 'For 2 locks, one key and a lether seale; 6s 0d 'For ye Bull teame making' in 1661 and in 1666 payment 'For ironworke for ye whipping post'.[8]

His will dated 26 February 1695, when he was eighty one years old is signed in a very shaky hand and he probably died soon after. Gunnis bequeathed his dwelling house, shop, stables and orchard to his son Philip Gunnis. Twenty shillings were to be paid at the age of twenty one to his grandson, William Gunnis, son of William Gunnis junior, deceased, late of Horncastle. His granddaughter Mary Gunnis was to receive ten shillings at the age of twenty one or upon her marriage, and another grandson, Francis Wright, five shillings at the age of eighteen. Presumably Philip Gunnis followed his father in the gunmaking business but further research is required to tease out the history of the earliest Louth gunmaker William Gunnis, and his family.

Chapman of Louth

A nine bore fowler by Monck (see Stamford section) in Moyses Hall museum, Bury St Edmunds, is furnished with a barrel bearing the stamp CHAPMAN LOUTH. The lock plate is struck with the name Monck (figures 12 and 13).

Left: figure 12: Barrel stamp of CHAPMAN, LOUTH, on a 9 bore fowler engraved MONCK on the lock plate (Moyses Hall Museum, Bury St Edmunds).

Below: figure 13: Detail of 9 bore fowler by Monck with barrel by Chapman (Moyses Hall Museum, Bury St. Edmunds).

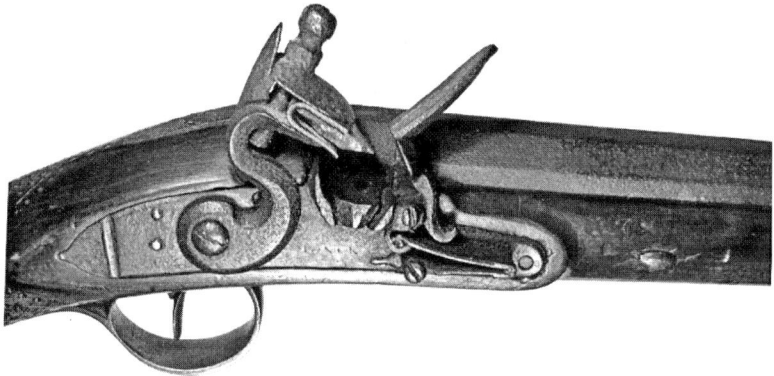

There were a number of Chapmans in London c.1714–1842; a Robert Chapman was at Boston, Lincs., c. 1826–49 and a John Chapman at Wisbech, Cambs., 1829. Thomas Monck completed his apprenticeship with William Newton of Grantham[9] in June 1771 and subsequently set up his own business in Stamford some twenty miles along the Great North Road. He is recorded there at Red Lion Square until c. 1830 and Mary Monck, probably his widow, was at the same address in 1834.

Bryan Tate fl. 1810–40 and Richard Tate, Louth and Horncastle (1803–57): fl. 1830–57

Richard Tate was born at Louth the son of Bryan Tate and Mary his wife, and was baptised 31 October 1803 at St James parish church. Bryan Tate is recorded in the trade directories 1810–40, but having been born in 1765 he is likely to have started his own business before the turn of the century. He had evidently been very successful and owned several properties and parcels of land, as well as his shop in Butcher Market, later known as the Cornmarket.[10] (figure 14).

figure 14: Shop of Bryan Tate, Butchers Market (now Cornmarket, Louth) as it is now.

In private hands there is a flint, box-lock pistol signed 'B. Tate Louth' within a simple oval outline. It measures 6 ¼ in overall with a brass frame and a steel barrel 1 ½ in long and ½ in bore. Deeply impressed on the left side of the frame is the name of the owner T ESPIN in bold capital letters. Thomas Espin FSA (1766–1822) born into a Lincolnshire farming family became an artist and teacher settling in Louth as headmaster of a charity school. He designed and built for himself a house in the Regency Gothic style called Priory Cottage (now a hotel and restaurant) and many of his drawings of Lincolnshire buildings were engraved and published.

A brass-barrelled flintlock blunderbuss, signed B.TATE on the lock, was advertised for sale in 2009 by Michael D. Long Ltd. Overall length 30 inches, a 14 inch barrel with cannon muzzle exhibiting a 1 ¼ bore. Full stocked with engraved brass mounts, a pineapple finial to the fore strap of the trigger guard, chequered wrist and a top mounted spring-loaded bayonet released by a thumb catch on top of the barrel tang.

When Richard opened his shop in 1830 his father was sixty five years old. The new business was also in Butcher Market and it would appear that Tate senior was not eager to let his son take over the family business, forcing the latter to set up in competition. Richard Tate moved to Horncastle (Lincs.) about 1847 to carry on his gunmaking business. According to the census of 1851 he was living at his shop in Millstone Street, now North Street. He is recorded in Whites trade directory of Lincolnshire, 1856, as a gunmaker and died the following year on Sunday 3 May 1857. There is a brief notice in the *Lincoln, Rutland and Stamford Mercury*, Friday 8 May 'at Horncastle in Millstone Street on 3rd instant Mr Rd. Tate Gunsmith aged 53 years'. A listing for Bryan Tate in the 1849 directory at Buttermarket, Horncastle is either an error or represents another son or other member of the family active for only a short time.[11] Richard's son, also called Richard, continued to occupy the same premises in Horncastle but as a watch and clock maker.[12]

A pair of screw barrel percussion pistols made by Richard Tate while still in Louth are illustrated in the *Guns Review* and for many years belonged to John Kendal Bourne, Lord of the Manor of Louth.[13]

figure 15: Bill dated 1839, from R. Tate; settled 21 April 1840 and signed Isabella Tate.

A bill preserved with them does not refer to the pistols but is written on headed notepaper 'Bought of R. Tate Gun and Pistol maker, Ironmonger and Bell hanger'. Ironmonger is crossed out and the initial R is inserted by hand, implying that he was using his father's bill heads. A vignette proclaims 'Patent Breeching and Percussion Locks' with a figure of a sportsman carrying a gun in one hand and a dead bird in the other with several dogs lying down and flanking more dead game birds. Made out to Mr Overton it covers a period from 25 February to 11 November 1839:

Feb	25	Fancy pad lock key	– 1-0
Mar	29	Gun cleaning	– 1-0
Sept	13	Stable lock repairing	– 1-6
	25	Gun cleaning	– 1-0
	26	Box caps	– 2-6
Oct	3	Gauge for powder and shot	– 0-6
	23	Stable lock new key	– 1-0
Nov	11	Spare rowling	– 0-6
			– 9-0

The bill is signed at the bottom 'Settled April 21 1840 I. Tate'; this was Isabella, Richard's wife. (figure 15).

A photograph of North Street (formerly Millstone Street) showing his son Richard Henry and his wife outside the shop in Horncastle is also reproduced in the *Guns Review*.[14]

In private hands there is a flint, box-lock pistol signed TATE within a simple oval outline on the left and LOUTH on the right. All steel it measures 6½ inches overall with a 1¼ inch barrel of 7/16 inch bore.

Michael Lill (1787/8–1844) fl. 1821–c. 1841

On 24 February 1817 Betsy the daughter of Michael and Sarah Lill was baptised at St James parish church, Louth. Sarah evidently weakened by childbirth died age 22 and was buried on 9 March of the same year. We

figure 16: 14 Upgate, Louth, as it is now, formerly the premises of Michael Lill, c.1821–1841. The three bayed building to the right, with pedimented windows, was originally the Mansion House and latterly the Mechanics Institute.

know that Michael Lill died in 1844 aged 57 therefore he was born in 1787–88 which following the usual apprenticeship, aged 14 to 21, he would have finished his term c.1808. However it is not until 1821 that we find him recorded in the trade directories running his own business at 14 Upgate (figure 16).

We can speculate that he was apprenticed to Bryan Tate but it is also possible he gained his training elsewhere, perhaps in London. We know that a John Lill was apprenticed to William Edwards of the Gunmakers Co. in 1741.[15] Lill is an unusual name it is likely that he was a kinsman, perhaps even the grandfather of Michael Lill.

At the time of the 1841 census Michael Lill is recorded, aged 50, at 14 Upgate with his housekeeper Elizabeth Stephenson, aged 20, and Edwin Dodson, aged 25 (q.v.). The Lill premises were handily situated next door to the Mansion House, the seat of local government, which would have brought a stream of influential local citizens and visitors past his front door.

A member of the town council himself he made his will 10 December 1842. The substantial legacies amounted to 'Less than £4000', Betsy his daughter being the principal beneficiary. She received 'all household furniture, earthenware, glass, china, plate linen, books and implements of household whatsoever' as well as profits and rents from his real estate and the income from £1000 to be invested in bonds and government securities, by the executors, Roger Sharply, a farmer of Great Carlton, John Porter, an attorney's clerk of Louth, and Joseph Larders the younger (grocer and provision dealer, Mercer Row, also of Louth. Edmund Cartwright, butcher of Louth (and Betsy's husband) was to receive the 'messuages or tenements, shop, slaughter house, stables, yard and other premised situate in Eastgate and Burnt-hill lane'. The witnesses were David Drakes and W H Faulding, but a codicil of 30 August 1843 was signed by Edwin Dodson (q.v.) and George West (q.v.). This altered a bequest of £50 to the Wesleyan Missionary Society to £10 for this organisation, £10 to Louth Auxiliary British and Foreign Bible Society, £10 to the British School, Louth and a further £10 to the Wesleyan Sunday School, Louth. In addition his housekeeper Elizabeth Stephenson was to receive 19 guineas.[16] Michael Lill died 11 May 1844, aged 57, and was buried 16 May in St Mary's cemetery.

A flintlock blunderbuss with spring bayonet on top of the barrel sold at Phillips auctioneers, 30 June 1983, as lot 22 (figure 17).
It was signed LILL on the lock plate and is probably the piece which belonged to the late John Bourne and sold at John Taylors auction rooms, Louth, 22 July 1981, lot 1298.

Another similar weapon is in the collection of the Louth Naturalists', Antiquarian and Literary Society, presented 1882. Measuring 29½ inches

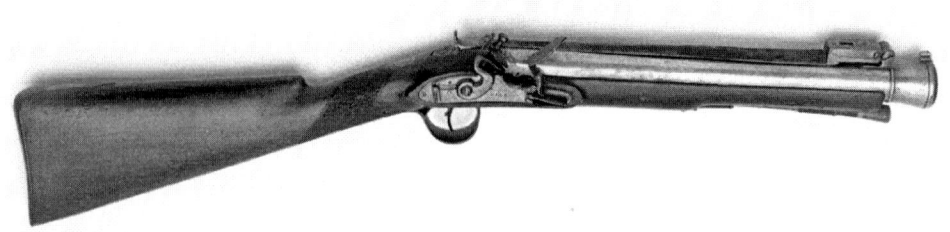

figure 17: Blunderbuss with folding bayonet, signed LILL on the lock plate; sold at auction, Phillips, 30 June 1983, lot 22.

long overall it has a brass cannon barrel, 13¾ inches long and 1¼ inch at the muzzle. Birmingham proof marks are struck on the breech and a barrel-makers mark of a letter I over a *fleur-de-lis*. All the furniture is brass and totally undecorated; the front strap of the trigger guard terminates in an acorn finial. Signed LILL on the lock plate, a sliding bolt safety operates at half-cock. The heel of the 'hammer' moves against a roller. When donated to the Louth museum it was said to have been used on the Louth-London stagecoach but if this is so it lacks any official marking which might confirm this story (figure 18).

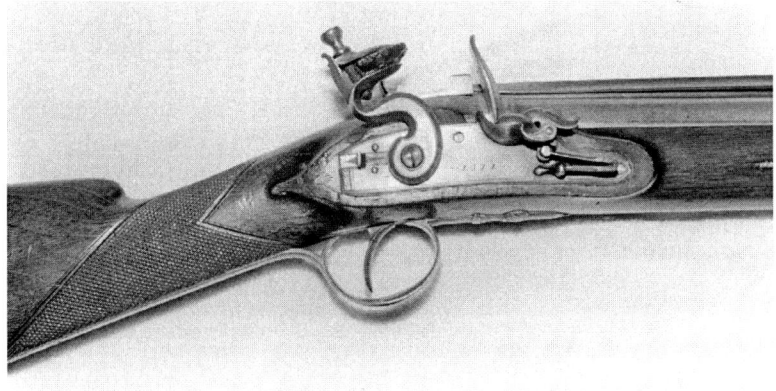

figure 18: Detail of a brass-barrelled blunderbuss with folding bayonet, signed LILL on the lock plate (Louth Naturalists, Antiquarian and Literary Society).

In private hands there is a brass cannon-barrelled blunderbuss which is blind stamped on the butt HMMC over L/5 indicating that this example was indeed used on the mail coach. The overall length is 31½ inches, the barrel 15¾ inches, ¹³⁄₁₆ inch at the muzzle. There is no bayonet or any mounting for such an adjunct. The lock plate is signed M. Lill, in script, and LOUTH in roman letters is boldly engraved on the breech end of the barrel. All the furniture is brass, with two pipes, decorated in crude and lively style, the trigger guard with a five petalled flower, the side plate with a shell pattern and the stepped extension of the butt plate with a trophy of arms, an oval shield exhibiting the union flag. The fore strap of the trigger guard terminates in a pineapple finial. (figure 19)

Still preserved in the HSBC (formerly Midland) Bank, Cornmarket, Louth, are three pistols each of which bear an oval escutcheon on the back of the butt, engraved L & L BANK, LOUTH., Founded in Lincoln 1833 the Lincoln & Lindsey bank originally occupied the Cornmarket premises, taken over by the Midland in 1913, the pistols were discovered during alterations to the building in 1982. A box-lock percussion pistol signed LILL on one side of the frame and LOUTH on the other is 6⅝ inch overall with a 2½ inch turn-off rifled barrel of ⅜ inch calibre. Birmingham proof and view marks are struck on the breech and a number 2 on the breech end of the barrel indicating that this was one of a pair of pistols (figure 20 and 21).

figure 19: Brass-barrelled, mail-coach blunderbuss, signed M. LILL, in script, on the lock plate, and LOUTH on the breech. Blind stamped on the butt HMMC L/5. Overall length 31 in; barrel 15 ¾ in and 1 ³⁄₁₆ in at the muzzle (private collection).

figure 20: Percussion pistol, signed LILL, LOUTH, used by the staff of the Lincoln and Lindsey Bank; rifled barrel 2 ½ in and 3/8 in calibre (HSBC Bank, Cornmarket, Louth).

figure 21: Upper side of pistol showing escutcheon engraved L & L BANK LOUTH (HSBC Bank, Louth).

The other two are identical side-hammer, percussion pistols, signed REILLY LONDON on the top flat of the smooth bore octagonal barrel and probably date to 1845–50. Joseph Charles Reilly and his son were active in High Holborn and then Oxford Street. Each has a belt hook on the left side, is 8 inches long overall, with a 2½ inch smooth-bore barrel of 9/16 inch bore, and a captive steel ramrod on a swivel. One is stamped 2 on the breech and barrel, the other 3, indicating that they were probably supplied en suite with a carbine or blunderbuss. A bullet mould, stamped 38, matches the Reilly pistols and a smaller one the Lill pistol and there is a small copper powder flask (figure 22).

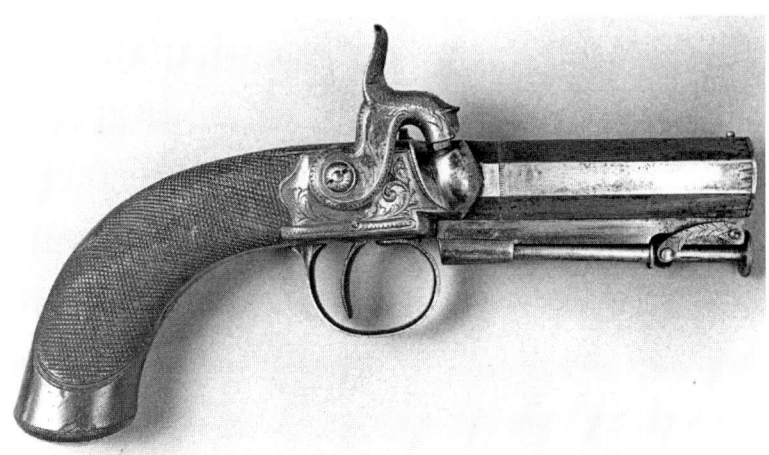

figure 22: Side-hammer percussion pistol, with belt hook on left side, and smooth bore barrel, signed REILLY LONDON on the top flat of octagonal barrel (HSBC Bank, Louth).

Tate and Lill

There was apparently a partnership between Tate and Lill, or perhaps one that was seriously contemplated and not carried through. A. Merwyn Carey records 'Tate and Lill' as active c.1800 in his *English, Irish and Scottish firearms makers* New York, 1967, though no firearms with the double signature are known. It is likely that any partnership would have followed the completion of Michael Lill's presumed apprenticeship with Bryan Tate, a period when Lill was gaining experience as a journeyman. We know that certainly by c.1820 Lill had set up on his own in Upgate. Whites directory for 1856 records Mrs. Mary Tate living in Upgate; the number is not given but if it was 14 these premises were then occupied by Edwin Dodson, successor to Lill. Another possible explanation of 'Tate and Lill' is a short lived partnership between either of the Tates and Michael Lill's (d. 1844) widow.

There are a number of English coins counterstamped 'Tate and Lill Louth'; like many others bearing the names of a multitude of craftsmen and retailers the marks were probably meant as a form of advertisement.

Thomas Sheppard, when director of Hull Museums, wrote a short article describing the Louth (and others from Thirsk) bringing the reader's attention to a number of examples which had probably been counterfeited.[17] Other countermarked coins are discussed in the Journal of the Arms and Society.[18]

Jonathan Kew (1808–67) fl. 1830–64 and Alfred Kew (1840–87) fl. 1864–87

Jonathan Kew was in business at Mercer Row from c.1834 (see below for foundation date) until 1867 and was probably the uncle of his successor, Alfred Kew. The latter's baptism is recorded in the parish registers of St James, Louth, 10 July 1840, son of William, a hairdresser, and Mary. A daughter Ellen had been baptised 16 March 1828 and a son Gilbert was registered 8 June 1843. The 1851 census lists a household which includes six children, the eldest, Marmaduke, 26, like his father a hairdresser and the youngest Gilbert, aged 7, also to become a hairdresser. Isabella, 28, was an infant school teacher; Ellen, 11, was still at school as were Frederick, 13 and Alfred, 9. Frederick in the 1861 census is listed as a professor of music, and Alfred, by then 20 years old, as a gun maker. On 24 October 1867 Alfred married Ann, the eldest daughter of Thomas Wilkinson Wallis.[19] Famous in his day he produced many virtuoso pieces of woodwork depicting dead game birds, minutely carved with every detail of their feathers.

In 1864 Jonathan Kew's shop at 27 Mercer Row (figure 23) changed its name to that of the new proprietor Alfred Kew and one assumes that the latter had been apprenticed to Jonathan. The latter's will dated 19 November 1864, when he must already have been ill or infirm devised all his personal estate to his wife Stachys (sic), she and a friend, Samuel Preston, were to be his executors. Jonathan died 19 August 1867, aged 59, and he was buried in London Road cemetery, Louth. The will was proved 5 October 1867 and the estate was valued at less than £450.

An advertisement for Alfred Kew in *White's* directory for 1872 describes him as 'gunmaker, single and double breech and muzzle-loading guns, dealer in rifles, revolvers and every other kind of pistol. Loaded cartridges of the best quality, 'pin' and 'central' fire. Fishing tackle in great variety. Superior pocket cutlery, and every article requisite for the sportsman' (see figure 24). This same advert gives the foundation date of the business as 1830.

figure 23: Kew's shop, later J P Hodgson, at 27 Mercer Row, Louth; as it is now.

ALFRED KEW, GUNMAKER.
SINGLE AND DOUBLE BREECH AND MUZZLE-LOADING GUNS.
Dealer in Rifles, Revolvers & every other kind of Pistol.

LOADED CARTRIDGES of the best quality—"Pin" and "Central" Fire.

FISHING TACKLE, in great variety. SUPERIOR POCKET CUTLERY; and every Article requisite for the Sportsman.

27, MERCER ROW, LOUTH.
ESTABLISHED 1830.

figure 24: Lincolnshire directory 1872; Alfred Kew, 27 Mercer Row, Louth.

Alfred Kew died 9 July 1887 aged 47 and was buried on 12 July. A notice in the *Louth and North Lincolnshire Advertiser*, Saturday 13 August 1887, informs the public that Mrs Kew begs to thank:

> ... the nobility and gentry for their past favours to her late husband and to inform them that the gun-making business established since 1830, has been taken by J. P. Hodgson (q.v.), who for many years has served in H M Corps of Armourers and is a native of this town, and who hopes by strict personal attention to business to elicit a fair share of patronage. All orders entrusted to him will be carefully carried out.

A six-shot, 32 calibre, bar-hammer, pepper-box signed 'Kew Louth' on the back strap can be assigned to Jonathan Kew. It measures 7¾ inches overall and the barrel cluster 3⅛ inches.

Edwin Dodson (1815–91) fl. 1841–91 and Frederick George Dodson (1834–99) partner 1868–91

An Edmund Dodson was born at Ashby-cum-Fenby (near Grimsby) c. 1780 and moved to Louth in the early 19th century where he worked as a cordwainer i.e. a boot and shoe maker. On 7 October 1811 he married Mary Milson at St James parish church in Louth. Their first child, Albert, was baptised in the same church 18 December 1812 and he followed his father in the craft of cordwainer while Edwin, baptised 7 May 1815 became a gunsmith and was himself followed in the trade by Frederick George Dodson, his brother, baptised 31 December 1834.

No record of indentures has been found but from the evident close links with Michael Lill, whose premises at 14 Upgate, Edwin Dodson took over, we can reasonably assume that Lill was Dodson's master. Lill retired 1840–41 and apparently remained in residence at Upgate until his death in 1844. Dodson, Lill and the latter's housekeeper are all recorded at this address during the 1841 census. Dodson witnessed a codicil to Lill's testament in 1843, along with George West, another gunsmith. (q.v.) It is perhaps surprising that no provision for Dodson appears in the will but it is likely that Dodson had already received the stock-in-trade and 'good-will' of the business as a gift or for a modest sum. An entry for Edwin Dodson, gunsmith, appears in Pigots directory for 1841.[20] On 12 February 1847 he advertised 'To gunmakers. Wanted a good workman in the above line of business–apply (if by letter, prepaid) to Edwin Dodson Gunmaker, Louth.'

figure 25: Birmingham proofed percussion bar hammer, pepper box pistol, signed DODSON, LOUTH.

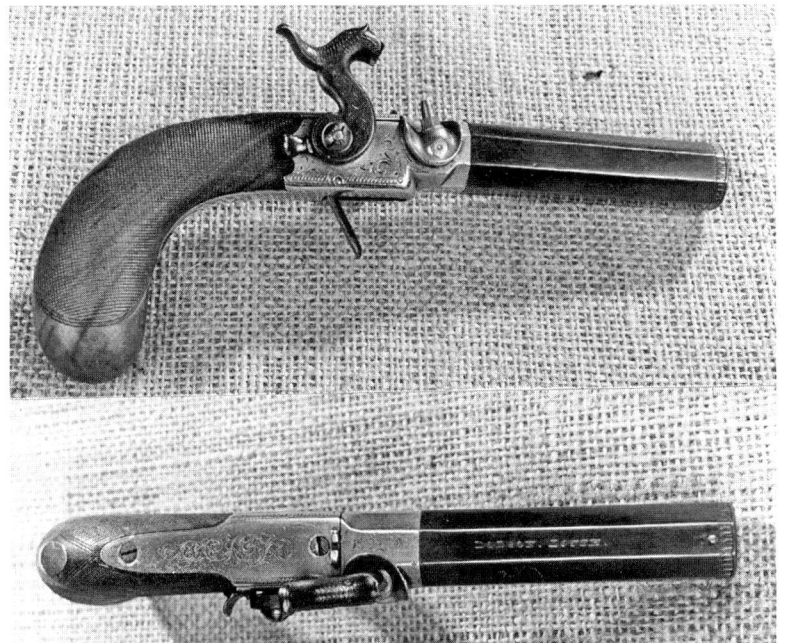

figure 26: Side-hammer percussion pistol, signed DODSON, LOUTH on top flat of octagonal barrel; German silver frame.

A Birmingham proved percussion, pepper-box pistol, c.1840–45, signed DODSON LOUTH is in a private collection (figure 25) and also a percussion pocket pistol with German silver frame is signed DODSON LOUTH on the top flat of the octagonal barrel. In fresh condition and with little sign of use it has a side-hammer and a concealed trigger which drops down when the pistol is cocked. (figure 26)

Thomas Wilkinson Wallis, carver and gilder, opened his own shop in Upgate in April 1844 and he tells us in his autobiography that his friend Edwin Dodson offered to loan him £10 to help him get started.[21] In September the same year Dodson saved Wallis' life when he got out of his depth swimming in the sea at Mablethorpe. Wallis was a keen shooter and was active in the rifle volunteers. He competed for the Queens Prize at Wimbledon in 1865, 1867 and 1868. His close links with the local gunmaking fraternity were cemented in 1867 when his eldest daughter Ann married Alfred Kew. (q.v.)[22]

A lithograph of Upgate and St James church was printed by Monkhouse of York in 1847 from a drawing by T. W. Wallis[23] (figure 27). On the left is Rileys grocers and tea dealers and next door but one is a two bay building with prominent windows inscribed DODSON GUNMAKER on the fascia board. The figure outside wearing a top hat and carrying a gun under his left arm is probably intended as a portrait of Edwin Dodson.

figure 27: Lithograph, 1847 by T. W. Wallis, of Upgate, Louth; Mr Dodson standing outside his shop at number 14.

In Hagar and Cos. commercial directory for 1849 Dodson is listed as a gunmaker, bell hanger and dealer in fishing tackle. Angling was ever popular and the demand for the installation of bells in shops, factories and households seems to have provided work for a great many gunsmiths and whitesmiths.

In the census, 30 March 1851, Dodson is recorded with his wife Elizabeth and Mary Broadley, a servant.[24] His brother Frederick George Dodson, aged 17, still at their father's house, 136 Market Place, is described as a gun maker's apprentice. The 1861 census records two men and two boys in Dodson's employment and living at 14 Upgate with his brother (and his wife, Henrietta Ann) and a 17 year old house servant. We learn from Teasdale Buckell that J P Hodgson (q.v.) was apprenticed to Dodson and he was probably one of these anonymous employees. Hodgson returned to Louth after army service to take over the business of Alfred Kew (q.v.)

In 1868 the year F G Dodson became a partner, the name of the business changed to E. and F. G. Dodson (figures 28 and 29).

Left: figure 28: Trade card of E Dodson of Louth; pre-1868.

Below: figure 29: Trade card of E and F G Dodson of Louth; post 1868.

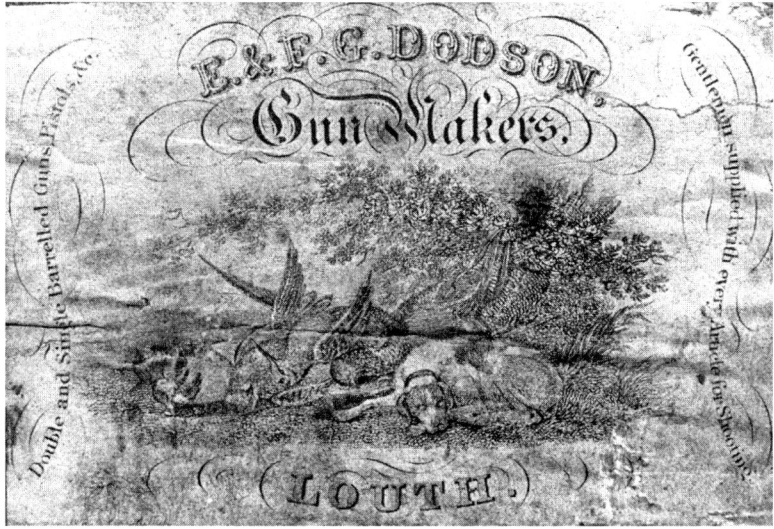

A farmer, Cornelius Stovin, tells us that in 1871 'I exchanged my old muzzle loader for a breech loader Dodson professed to charge seven pounds ten shillings and take off fifty shillings for the old one so I had to part with a five pound note'.[25] The wording of the advertisements both in *White's* 1872 and 1882 directories for Lincolnshire is identical 'E and F G Dodson, Gunsmiths and Bell hangers, Dealer in Fishing Tackle, Fishing Rods etc. 14 Upgate, Louth.'

In 1852 the Mansion House, next door, was put up for sale and bought by the Louth Mechanics Institution for £830. This money, and more besides which was spent on alterations, was raised in a three day bazaar organised by Dodson's friend T. W. Wallis, who since 1851 had been curator of the Institution, which, established in 1834, had originally occupied the top floor of the Public Building in Mercer Row.

Carey (who confused Louth in Lincolnshire with that in Ireland) tells us that he made 'cased percussion sea-captains pistols'.[26] Since Grimsby an expanding port was not far away a trade with local seafarers is not unlikely, especially with a lack of any significant gun-making tradition in that town.

An interesting find was made in 1983 when a six-shot revolver, in a case, was discovered in the cupboard of an old 'farmhouse in North Lincolnshire'. Described as a pin-fire the photograph rather suggests that it was either a rim-fire or centre-fire pistol, somewhat like an Adams revolver.[27] The trade label is that of E. and F. G. Dodson, but except for the absence of E DODSON LATE LILL found on the early labels the central design and letter press are essentially the same.

Edwin died at Upgate, aged 75, Thursday 23 April 1891, 'after a short illness'. He was buried in the London Road cemetery, Louth, on 27 April. His brother carried on the business until his own death, aged 64, Friday 30 March 1899, and he also was buried in the London Road cemetery.[28]

Two 12 bore double-barrelled hammer guns signed E and F G Dodson were sold from the collection of John Bourne, 22 July 1881, lot 1304 bearing the serial numbers 894 and 2022 and lot 1312 in a case.

George West, of Louth and Retford (1822–80), fl. 1848–80, and his successors

George West was born in 1822 at Waltham, then a small village near Grimsby but now almost encompassed by the latter's urban sprawl. He was baptised at All Saints, Waltham,[29] 10 January, and three or four years later, his parents, Edward and Mary West, moved to the thriving market town of Louth, some ten miles to the south of Grimsby which at this time was still quite a small riverside settlement. It grew only with the development of the North Sea fishery, stimulated by the expanding railway network.

The census returns for 1841 record George West as the eldest child, aged 18, living with his parents and siblings. His father, aged 50, was a bricklayer but George is described as a gunmakers apprentice and the eldest daughter Mary West as a dressmaker.[30] No indenture has been discovered, but assuming he started the usual seven year apprenticeship at the age of fourteen in 1836 then he was likely to have been working for Michael Lill, gunmaker, at 14 Upgate Street, Louth. Some three years later at the early age of 52 Lill retired and was succeeded by Edwin Dodson at the same address. A codicil of the last will and testament of Michael Lill, dated 13 August 1843, is signed by two witnesses, Dodson and George West who reached his majority in that year. Dodson had probably been Lill's foreman and would have taken over his former employers apprentices and workmen.

Aged twenty one West, having completed his term, was free to marry Mary Ann Howlett on 19 November 1843 at Louth Wesleyan chapel. As West of Spital Street, Louth, he is described in the register as a gun maker, and his father-in-law, John Howlett, as a tailor. The witnesses were John Pinder and Martha Howlett. West remained with Dodson until March 1847 and then set up business at 60 Eastgate, an address also listed as Fish Market, and in the 1851 census as 11 Market Place. (figure 30)

At the time of West's departure Dodson advertised in the *Lincoln, Rutland and Stamford Mercury*, 12 February 1847, 'To gunsmiths. Wanted a good workman in the above line of business. Apply (if by letter prepaid) to Edwin Dodson, Gunmaker, Louth'.

West appears in the trade directories at 60 Eastgate from 1848. In the 1851 census he is described as a 'gunmaker and bell hanger'[31] and had three children, a son George, aged four and two daughters, Amelia (6), and Henrietta (2). Living with him at 11 Market Place was Ebenezer Lingard, aged 17, born at Fotherby in 1834, an apprentice he had taken on in 1848.

The survival rate of Lincolnshire firearms is not high but three items with West's Louth address are known. One is a 110 bore, Birmingham proved,

figure 30: The premises of George West, 60 Eastgate, Louth, as they are now.

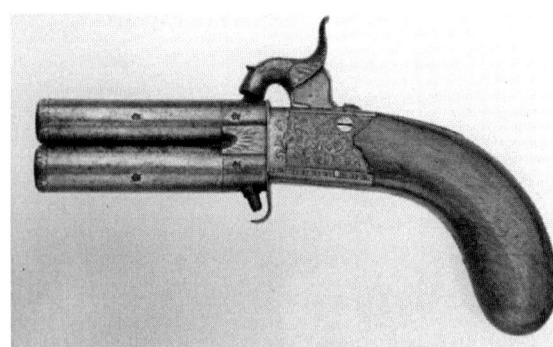

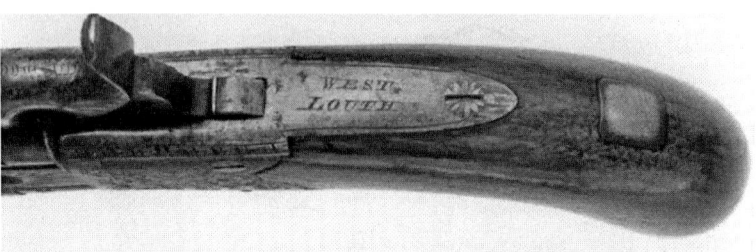

figure 31 (left) & figure 32 (below): Two barrel, turn-over percussion pistol, signed WEST LOUTH on top of frame.

turnover pocket pistol, overall length 6¾ inches, barrels 2⅜ inches, signed on the back strap WEST LOUTH (figures 31 and 32). The second is a double-barrelled, eight bore, back action, percussion gun signed simply WEST on the lock plate and LOUTH on the spine, overall length 51½ inches, the barrels 35⅛ inches. The third was a percussion over-and-under boxlock, turn-over pistol from the collection of John Bourne sold as lot 1282 at Louth 22 July 1981.

Despite being in proximity to his former master, as well as Kew in Mercer Row, business was evidently good. When he moved to Retford (Notts.) in late 1861 or early 1862[32] to take over the business (established in 1827 by Thomas Slingsby),[33] he took with him three workmen. Unfortunately their names are not recorded but one of these would have been George West junior, an apprentice to his father.

Retford was a very promising place in which to settle, a market town and like Grantham and Stamford on the Great North Road. It was also by then on the railway route from London to the north. There would have been a good passing trade as well as potential custom from the great aristocratic estates in the vicinity, which gave the area the nickname of 'the Dukeries'. Welbeck alone, belonging to the Duke of Portland, employed fifty keepers so there were good prospects for the sale of quality guns to the great landed proprietors and work-a-day guns to their extensive staff along with large quantities of ammunition. This was the period when the breech-loading shotgun was establishing its dominance in the gun trade.

figure 33: West and Son, Market Place, Retford c.1920.

In the census of 1871 West was living with his family at Market Place (figure 33). Also recorded is George Preston, 23, a gun maker, born at Louth,[34] no doubt one of the staff brought to the new establishment in 1861–62 when Preston might have been at the start of his apprenticeship.

A typical trade card of the period shows a sportsman with gun raised and a dog, running across a log over a stream, entitled 'G West Gunmaker etc. Grove Street, Retford, Gentlemen supplied with every article for shooting. Eleys cartridges supplied. Central Fire Breech Loading Guns and Rifles with the latest improvements made to order. Emigrants supplied'. An advertisement, c. 1870, proclaims him as 'manufacturer of Breech-loading and Muzzle-loading Guns and Rifles of every description. Wholesale and Retail dealer in all kinds of sporting ammunition. Breech Loaders made to special order from 7 to 30 guineas, on the most approved principles, which cannot be surpassed by any house in the trade for price.' At the bottom, a final note 'Emigrants supplied on the most liberal terms' which implies a considerable outflow from the local population to the colonies or the U.S.A.

West died, aged 57, on 10 January 1880, an event noted in the Retford and Gainsborough Times on Friday 16 January, and he was buried in Retford cemetery where a simple headstone can still be seen. Shortly afterwards the name of the business changed to E West (Gunmakers) under the ownership of Eliza West (figures 34 and 35), George's widow. Frank West[35] their son was eventually to take over the running of the shop so it seems that George the eldest son of West's first marriage had not survived.[36] Eliza was in semi-retirement by 1904 and she moved to Leicester in 1908 where she died 'after a long and painful illness' 7 February 1914 aged 71 and was buried in Braunton churchyard.[37] The shop then changed its style to West and Son, Gunmakers, The Square, Retford.

figure 34: Bill issued by E. West, Grove street, Retford, 1895 for powder, wads, amberite cartridge and alterations to a breechloaders's gun lock.

figure 35: Bill of E. West, Grove street, Retford,1902-1903 for a .410 wad punch, horn piece fitted to the stock and ½ lb. of Schultz powder.

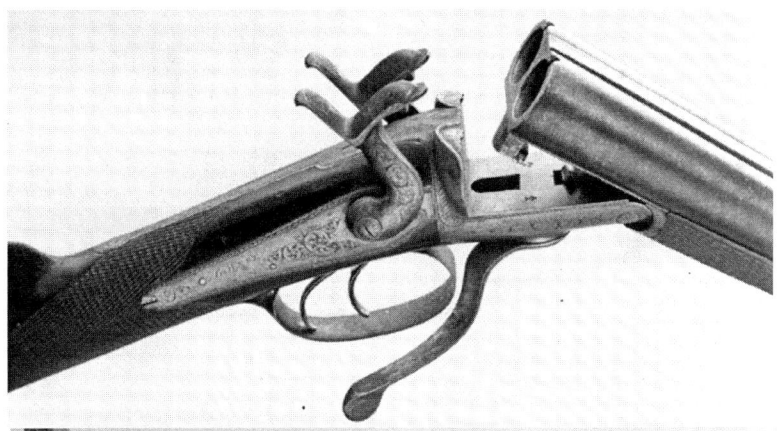
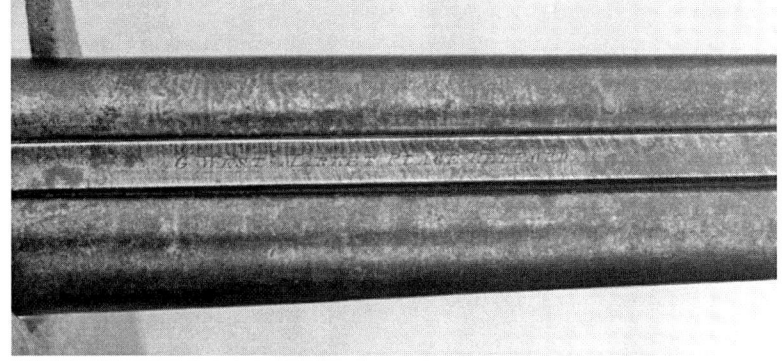

figure 36 (a & b): Back action 12 bore, pin-fire, double barrel shotgun signed G. WEST on the lock plate and G WEST MARKET PLACE RETFORD on the spine.

A number of breech-loaders by West of Retford have been seen, dating between about 1870 and 1910. A back-action 12 bore, pin-fire, double barrelled gun is signed G WEST on the lock plate and G WEST MARKET PLACE RETFORD on the spine (figure 36). A variety of hammer guns are signed G WEST GROVE ST RETFORD, G WEST or WEST RETFORD.

In December 1910 Frank West had received an order by telegram for one thousand cartridges to be delivered to Allerton station for Prince Nicholas[38] of Greece who was then staying at Retford Abbey home of the Saviles. A letter subsequently sent from Paris requested him to send the bill to the prince in Athens and on 4 May 1911 a cheque for £6 5s duly arrived.

Accompanying this letter from the prince's aide was a testimonial conferring on West '*le titre de des fournisseur de son Altesse Royale*'.[39] A double page advertisement subsequently published in a trade directory displays the coat of arms of his royal patron and a very impressive list of the aristocracy and gentry (figure 37). The foundation date of the firm is given as 1858 which is curious since George West was certainly in business by himself by 1848 but was in Retford only from 1861–62. A notice in the Shooting Times 22 November 1919 (repeated 27 December), reads as follows:

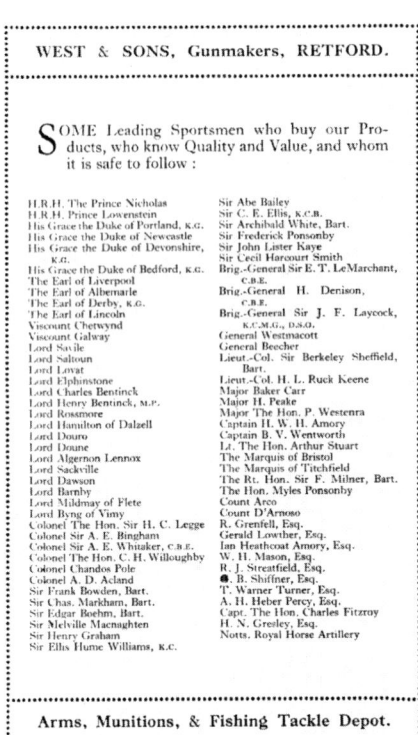

figure 37: Trade directory, advertisement c.1910 for West and Son, showing arms of Prince Nicholas of Greece and list of patrons.

GUNS GUNS GUNS Before buying a gun send for our illustrated folder of the new B.S.A. 12 bore double barrel hammerless shotgun at 7 guineas. Don't write the company; they will not deal with you. For further particulars write Messrs. West and Son, Gunmakers, 25 The Square, Retford. Established over 60 years.

The number should be 26 not 25 and this remained the address until 1834 when the business moved to 10 Bridge Gate and Frank West was succeeded by his son Peter. From 1955 until 1969, West and Son was at 2 Moorgate, then West and Son Ltd was set up at Mansfield Woodhouse as toolmakers and precision engineers.[40] The retirement of Peter West in 1969 ended more than 120 years family involvement in the gun trade.

Henry Godsall of Gloucester, London and Louth

Peter Hawker refers to Godsall in his *Instructions to Young Sportsmen* in 1833[41] 'Henry Godsall, who worked nine years for him [Lancaster][42] and eight for Joe Manton, has just established himself, as barrel filer and finisher at 86, Oxford Street, where he showed me some of his improvements for making more perfect the screws of breechings, and putting well together the barrel, of double guns. On his plan however badly the barrels may be filed outside, they must be mathematically true in the position of their cylinders.'[43]

Blackmore describes Godsall as a gun barrel maker at Turk's Head Yard, Oxford Street, 1836–41 and at 86 Oxford Street, 1840–53. He evidently left London and retired north and he appears in *White's* directory for Lincolnshire, 1856, living in Grimsby Road, Louth. The 1861 census describes him as a retired gunsmith, aged 73, still at the Grimsby Road address. His place of birth was Gloucestershire and his wife Mary, aged 54, was Lincolnshire born. Kelly's Post Office directory, 1861, more specifically gives his home as Gloucester Terrace,[44] Grimsby Road. The *Louth and North Lincolnshire Advertiser* 23 April 1864 briefly noted his death 'At Louth, on the 21st instant, Mr Henry Godsall, 76 years'. There is a slight discrepancy in the 1841 census, while he was working in London, when he is said to have been 50, this would make his birth year 1791 rather than 1788 as implied by his obituary notice.

A George Brider was apprenticed to him as recorded in the 1841 census when he was aged 15. He is listed as a gun barrel and implement maker at various London addresses from 1851 until 1879 (Blackmore *A dictionary of London gunmakers* 1986).

The Henry Godsall recorded at Lower College Lane, Gloucester, 1797–1815 was no doubt his father.[45] A pair of pistols is known, reckoned to be c. 1780, by Henry Godsall of Gloucester[46] and a duck gun signed Godsall of c. 1800, with a 79 inch barrel were sold at Christies in 2002 (Antique Arms and Armour, 18 July, lot 205). It may be noted that a Major Godsal (sic), Eton, contributed a 'Military rifle, with 'Godsal' Rifle Action' as item 5203 of the Royal Naval Exhibition at Chelsea, 1891; see page 486 of the catalogue.

Ebenezer Lingard, of Louth and Grimsby, born c. 1834, fl. 1862–92

In the 1851 census at Louth Ebenezer Lingard is recorded aged 17 living with George West, gunmaker, to whom he was apprenticed. Some time about 1862–67 he started his own business in Trinity Lane, Louth, described as a bell hanger but presumably dealing as a gunsmith too. By 1864 he was at 26 Aswell Lane and in 1872 he can be found in the Grimsby trade directories at 150 Victoria Street and from c.1876–82 at 35 Victoria Street West. The style changes from c. 1892 to Ebenezer Lingard and Co. by which time the founder was probably retired or dead, and now at 154 Victoria Street. The latest listings are for 1907 and 1908 at 144 Victoria Street.

A Thomas Lingard, very probably his son, is at Queens Street, Grimsby, 1882. It is an unusual surname so it seems highly likely that Noah Lingard, gun lock maker, noted by Bailey and Nie, at Wednesbury, Staffs, in 1849, was a kinsman, possibly he was the father of Ebenezer.

Jesse Parker Hodgson (1841–1923) fl. 1887–1911 and Alfred Arthur Hodgson (1881–?) fl. 1911–c. 1919

Jesse Parker Hodgson was born in 1841 on 9 April and baptised on the nineteenth of that month in St James parish church, Louth. His father Robert Parker Hodgson, was a tailor in the town, born at Hogsthorpe (Lincs.), and his mother a straw bonnet maker.[47]

Teasdale Buckell[48] tells us that J P Hodgson of Louth was apprenticed to William Edwin Dodson which no doubt refers to Edwin Dodson of 14 Upgate Louth but there is no other evidence the latter had the additional christian name of William. Assuming the usual term started at the age of 14 he would have completed his seven years in 1862. Almost immediately he must have headed south, for Buckell further states that he worked for the Royal Small Arms Factory (Enfield) and the Corps of Armourers in 1863.[49]

According to his obituary Hodgson was in the Corps (from 1896 the Army Ordnance Dept. Armourers) for some 24 years, ten with the Lincolnshire regiment (10th Foot) and fourteen with the Durham Light Infantry. Army service took him to China, Japan, the Cape and India and he 'was the first to teach the Japs the use of the rifle and to do the necessary repairs'.[50] On leaving the army he took over the business of Alfred Kew at 27 Mercer Row (figure 38). In 1887 Mrs Kew announced the change of ownership in the *Louth and North Lincolnshire Advertiser*, 13 and 20 August, and Hodgson inserted his own advertisement into the *Louth Standard* 14 January 1888:

figure 38: Mercer Row, Louth, c.1918. Hodgson's shop (number 27, formerly that of Mr Kew) is a two-bayed building with an alley immediately to the left, and a ten bayed building beyond. A rectangular sign outside the shop reads HODGSON SPORTING GOODS etc.

Established 1840. Jesse Parker Hodgson Gun Maker at 27 Mercer Row, Louth wishes to thank his numerous customers for the support they have given him during the short time he has been in business, and hopes for a continuance of the same.

A large quantity of cutlery, walking sticks, fishing tackle, all requisites for shooting kept in stock.

All repairs to guns, fishing rods, and general repairs neatly executed. Sticks mounted in silver, white metal, buck horn, stag horn, etc in the best style.

NB. A few guns and revolvers (old stock) at greatly reduced prices.

The foundation date is wrongly given, it should of course be 1830. An extensive description appears in the *Gazette of Industries of the Eastern Counties*, c. 1892, and like his first advert an engraving of a double barrelled shotgun heads the piece:

Jesse Parker Hodgson, Gunmaker etc 27 Mercer Row. The principal establishment in the trade in the town of Louth is that of Mr Jesse Parker Hodgson, Gunmaker and Dealer in sporting requisites, which is situated at 27 Mercer Row. This flourishing business is an old established one having been founded in the year 1830, and was long carried on with great success by Mr Kew; but since the concern has been in the hands of its present proprietor it has been greatly increased, both in extent and importance, mainly by his strict devotion to business and his well known enterprise. The premises occupied are three stories in height, and have a good frontage, with a capital window, in which a high class display of guns, pistols and revolvers, and other weapons and sporting appliances is always maintained. The shop is of good size, and contains a large stock of guns of all descriptions used for sporting purposes, from the ponderous duck or punt gun to the elegant rook rifle, as well as revolvers and other defensive weapons, fishing rods and tackle, walking sticks, sword-sticks, cutlery, etc etc. Over the shop there is a well-appointed workshop which is furnished with all the necessary appliances of the trade, and guns of all descriptions are here made to order. In addition to making and repairing fowling pieces etc Mr Hodgson also undertakes the repair of fishing tackle, tennis rackets, cricket bats, and athletic or sporting requisites of all kinds. The manufacture of cartridges is also an important brand of this business, and those made of 'smokeless and black powder' are especially in demand and a speciality of Mr Hodgson's. He also supplies cartridges (four wads) from 7s 6d per hundred. He enjoys the patronage of the chief sportsmen of the district and is on all hands much esteemed for his personal good qualities, as well as for the soundness of his work. Mr Hodgson served in HM Corps of Armourers for a period of twenty four years with great credit during which time he had responsible positions in several arsenals and regiments under the English and Indian governments.

The 1891 census describes Hodgson as a gun and fishing tackle maker and the age of both himself and his wife as 49. Living with them were his eldest son, Henry Parker Hodgson, aged 19, 'gunsmiths assistant', a daughter aged 13 a young son Alfred Arthur, aged 10.

On a memorandum sheet with printed heading is written what appears to be the draft for an advertisement:

> J P Hodgson. Gunmaker and Cycle Manufacturer etc. Central Cycle Stores 27 Mercer Row Louth. A choice selection of guns–Hammerless, Ejectors, Hammer Guns, Rifles, Muzzle Loaders etc. Cartridges a speciality.
> Bicycles The Luda (our own make) and by best leading makers. Latest Novelties in Lamps, Bells and all Accessories from the Stanley Show. Repairs by experienced workmen. A trial solicited. See window for Xmas Novelties.

On the reverse, is a faintly printed advertisement for Schultze gunpowder:

> the original smokeless powder. Quick ignition. High velocity. Great Penetration. Regular. Powerful. Safe. Highest Honours wherever exhibited. London 1885. Chicago 1893. California 1894. Antwerp 1894. Milan 1894. Atlanta 1895 ... Pigeon Shooting. Schultze has won all National and International Championships on both sides of the Atlantic ... International Meeting Hurlingham and the Gun Club June 1896. Schultze the Champion Sporting Powder.

An advertisement in Bennett's Business Directory of 1898 emphasises his cycle making and retailing, a major activity for many provincial gunsmiths at the turn of the century.

> J. P. Hodgson Gun Maker, Fishing Tackle Dealer and Manufacturer of the Suda[51] cycle, 27 Mercer Row, Louth. Cycle agencies for Humber, Raleigh, Excelsior and all leading makers. A large assortment of accessories. Repairs neatly executed.

In contrast an advertisement in the *Louth and North Lincolnshire Advertiser*, 14 December 1898 concentrates on the firearms and sporting guns:

> J. P. Hodgson, Gunmaker etc at 27, Mercer Row, Louth, for Guns, Rifles, Revolvers and all Sporting Requisites. Double Barrel 12 bore, Central Fire, Breech Loading Guns (fully guaranteed) from £3. Cartridges a Speciality. Gun cases, Cartridge Bags, Game Carriers, Dog Slips, Hockey Sticks and Balls, Footballs, Skates etc in Great Variety.

An obituary and photograph appeared in the *Louth Standard* on 27

January 1923 (figure 39), which tells us that he died on 21 January, aged 81 and had apparently retired aged 70, i.e. in 1911. By this time his eldest son was dead[52] and the business was taken over by his youngest son Alfred Arthur Hodgson. J. P. Hodgson is described as a keen Freemason into which society he had been initiated while in India. He was a director of the Corn Exchange Co. and an ardent Conservative, being a member and shareholder of the Cannon Street Conservative Club. A regular attendee of the Louth Bowling Club he had played until a year before his death and was known on the green as 'The Colonel'.

The funeral service was held at the deceased's residence, 5 Priory Terrace, attended by family and friends, representatives of the Lindsey Lodge of Freemasons, the Conservative Club and Bowls Club. His son A A Hodgson, aged 42, is described as 'of Cambridge' so must himself have relinquished the family business by then.[53] Probate was granted 7 March 1923 to A. A. Hodgson, gunsmith, and Philip Francis Bultitude, retired Army Warrant Officer; the value was £974.

In the parish registers of St Michael, Louth, 7 January 1907 the baptism is recorded of Mary Hodgson daughter of A. A. Hodgson, gun and cycle maker. He and his wife Mary Louise resided at 'Pendover', Eastgate, Louth. Bennett's directory for 1911 records A. A. Hodgson at 27–29 Mercer Row and residing at 3 High Holme Villas, High Holme Road, Louth. Between

figure 39: Jesse Parker Hodgson from the *Louth Standard* 27 January, 1923.

figure 40: Breech-loading shotgun, signed J P Hodgson on the side plate.

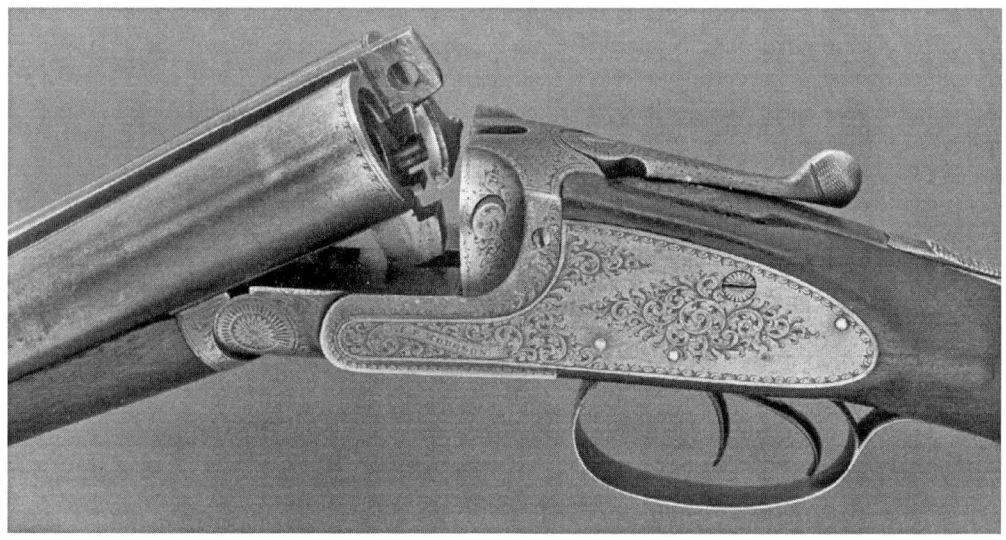

1913 and 1919 the trade directories list A. A. Hodgson still in business at 27 and 29 Mercer Row.

Guns retailed by Hodgson can be found bearing the W B stamp of William Baker (1858-1934) of Birmingham. According to Tate, between 1889-1924 'Baker built guns based on his own patents for the London and provincial trade from workshops first at Snow Hill and later from 7 Bath Street. The most commonly encountered are sidelock side-by-sides with inexpensive coil-spring lock work built by Vickers of Crayford and J P Hodgson of Louth. Less frequently over-unders built for Hanson and Hussey and G and S Holloway come to light.[54] (figure 40).

Stamford

John Ed(g)son and David Ed(g)son fl. c.1780–1821

In 1765, William Edson (or Edgson) arrived in Grantham, a 'foreigner' he was admitted to the freedom of his trade by paying the usual fine of £20 and established himself in competition with the Newton workshop.[55] John Edgson, who had been apprenticed to his father completed his indentures in 1773 and subsequently set up in business in nearby Stamford. An advertisement in the *Lincoln, Rutland and Stamford Mercury*, 27 August 1790, reads as follows:

> John Edgson, Gun Maker, Red Lion Street. Takes this opportunity of returning thanks for the encouragement he has received in the above trade; and begs leave to inform his friends, and the public, he has now completed a choice assortment of guns, both double and single, with twisted and plain steel barrels, made up in the neatest manner, which he intends selling on the most reasonable terms; with every article in the gun and cutlery branches. He also bores gun-barrels according to the latest improvements. NB. Fine powder, patent shot etc.

John and David Edgson are listed in the directories c.1810 then John only in 1815[56], which is curious assuming David is the son of John. Possibly David and John were brothers. Thomas Monck moved into David Edgson's shop, Red Lion Square in 1817 (see below).

Jon Culverhouse, curator of Burghley House, near Stamford, informed the editor that there are 'seven flintlock smooth-bore militia carbines, modelled on the Baker rifle, all by Edgson of Stamford, c.1815' in the collection there.

Thomas Monck senior (b. 1745/6–d. 1830) fl. 1773–1825; Thomas Monck junior (b. 1777/8–d. 1830) fl. c.1801–30; and Thomas Bingham Monck fl. 1832–57

Monck became an apprentice to William Newton of Grantham immediately after the latter attained his freedom. Monck himself was granted his freedom[57] 19 June 1771 and is recorded at his shop in Red Lion Square, Stamford from c.1797. Assuming 84 is the correct age recorded in the local newspaper in 1830 this would make his age in 1771 as 25 or 26 and indicate his apprenticeship started at 18 or 19 years old, rather later than usual.

The addresses of Thomas Monck senior and junior are somewhat confusing and in 1817 (*Stamford Mercury* 10 Oct.) a Mr Monck gunsmith, presumably the son, is reported as moving to the shop of David Edgson in Red Lion Square. In the same year Hannah, the wife of Monck senior, died aged 70 (*Stamford Mercury* 13 June 1817). Thomas Monck of Red Lion Square is reported in 1823 (*Stamford Mercury* 29 August) as having been in business fifty years i.e. he must have set up on his account in 1773.

In the *Lincoln, Rutland and Stamford Mercury* 20 April 1825 when he would have been aged about 75 he is evidently in a state of bankruptcy or indebtedness:

> Mr Thomas Monck's Assignment. Whereas Thos. Monck, the elder, of Stamford in the County of Lincoln, gunsmith, hath by indenture bearing the date the 21st day of April instant, assigned over his personal estate and effects to Charles Reesby, of Stamford, aforesaid, baker, in trust for the equal benefit of all his creditors ... By order of the Assignees, Stamford 28 April 1825 T. H. Jackson.

His death occurred in 1830 (*Stamford Mercury* 26 March) aged 84 when he is described as warden of Lord Burghley's hospital; Monck's year of birth must therefore have been 1745–46.

Thomas Monck junior married a Miss Pulford 12 January 1801 (*Stamford Mercury* 16 January) and in 1804 he subscribed to the local Yeomanry and received payment for repair of arms for the Stamford infantry (*Stamford Mercury* 20 January and 16 November 1804). As well as guns he was also selling sporting dogs (11 October 1805, 1 August 1806) and 10 July 1812 offers a Manton gun for sale. Advertising for a journeyman (19 September 1817) he moved to Red Lion Square as recorded above in October 1817 (*Stamford Mercury* 10 October), his former shop in the High Street being occupied by a Mr Allatt, a brazier (13 February 1818). Monck's daughter died aged 17 (*Stamford Mercury* 11 September 1818) and in December of the same year shot chargers and knives are stolen from his shop (11 December). Thomas Lightfoot, Thomas Edgson and John Marriot are acquitted of stealing from Mr Monck (*Stamford Mercury* 22 January 1819).

Evidently he wished to educate his family to the highest standards and advertised in 1819 for a classics tutor (16 April 1819). An advertisement at the beginning of 1820 indicates that he repaired percussion guns (*Stamford Mercury* 7 January) and in August he was seeking a workman (*Stamford Mercury* 18 August). On 29 December of the same year Monck and Co of Red Lion Square advertised a patent alarm pistol and pocket book pistol for security. On 6 September 1822 the *Stamford Mercury* recorded the marriage at Edenham of the eldest son of Thomas Monck, gunsmith, to Miss Scoles of Grimsthorpe. Two years later Thomas Monck junior, gunsmith, cutler and engraver moved to Ironmonger Street (*Stamford Mercury* 13 August 1824) and it is announced 3 June that:

> Thomas Monck junior gunsmith, cutler and engraver Red Lion Square, Stamford, returns his sincere thanks to his friends for the liberal encouragement he has experienced since his commencement in business; and takes this opportunity of informing them he has taken his father's business in the Red Lion Square where he intends carrying it on in all its trades, and hopes by strict and unremitting attention to all orders, he may be favored with, to merit their future patronage. PS. A handsome assortment of the best London cutlery, at reasonable prices.

Shortly afterwards yet another move is recorded in the *Stamford Mercury* 7 April 1826:

> To gentlemen Sportsmen. Thomas Monck jun. Gun-maker etc, St. Johns Street, returns his sincere thanks to his friends and the public in general for the favors conferred on him and takes this opportunity of informing them he has removed from the situation in Red Lion Square to the shop lately occupied by Mr Chambers, shoe maker, St. Johns Street, where he intends carrying on the above business in all its trades ... T. M. has on sale a handsome assortment of Double and Single Barrel Guns, and every article requisite for the sportsman, at the most reasonable prices PS. Gentlemen sending guns and parcels by carriers or others, will be pleased to direct them for Thomas Monck jun. St. Johns Street.

On 3 August 1827, he advertised as gun and pistol maker of St Johns Street and on 8 August 1828 at the same address he offered a selection of percussion guns. On 28 August of the same year Monck proclaimed himself agent for patent Swiss capsules. On 29 October 1830 the *Stamford Mercury* announced Monck's death at the early age of 52, this was only seven months after the death of his father.

Extracts from the *Stamford Mercury* index at the Stamford Museum enable us to follow the progress of the Monck family of gunsmiths. Mary Monck, his widow, announced her intention of carrying on the business (19 November 1830) but their son Thomas Bingham Monck took charge of the shop in St Johns Street as appears from the advertisement 10 August 1832 when he thanks the public for their support and indicates he has a license to sell game. He offers a pair of pointer bitches for sale, 19 October 1832. As regards the Bingham name it is interesting to note that Richard Bingham, former baker of Peterborough, died aged 81 at the house of Mr Monck, gunsmith (*Stamford Mercury* 26 November 1824).

By 1839 taxidermy has been added to the services offered:

> To the Nobility, Gentry and Sportsmen. T B Monck, gun-smith, St. Johns Street, Stamford, returns his most grateful thanks to his numerous friends for the very distinguished patronage he has received in the above business, and begs to assure them it will be his study to merit their future support, by a strict attention to all orders submitted to his care, which, from his long practice and experience, he feels fully competent in undertaking. T. B. directs the attention of gentlemen to the stock of new guns which he has furnished for the present season; also a fresh supply of gunpowder, shot, caps, wadding and every other article requisite for the sportsman. Bird and animal stuffing neatly executed

(*Lincoln, Rutland and Stamford Mercury* 30 August 1839).

In the same newspaper for 16 February 1838 a one guinea reward is offered for finding a dog lost from the rectory at Cottesmore and returning it either direct to the rectory or to 'Mr Monck, gunsmith, Stamford'. T B Monck appears in the trade directories until c.1857.[58]

A late 18th or early 19th century trade card demonstrates an enlargement of the business into clocks and watches:

> Thomas Monck, Stamford; Takes the liberty to acquaint his friends, and the public in general, that he has engaged his brother Edward Monck clock and watchmaker, late journeyman to James Wilson; and that he intends carrying on the clock and watch-making business ....

Wilson, a gold and silversmith, clock and watchmaker and engraver 'near All Saints church, Grantham', advertised his new stock in the *Lincoln, Rutland and Stamford Mercury*, 13 March 1789,[59] which included buckles, spurs and fine cutlery and a great variety of clocks and watches sold and repaired, spring and weight driven and clocks, musical clocks etc.

Mr Monck, gunsmith, clock and watchmaker, the High Street, advertised in the *Stamford Mercury* 5 November, 1802, offering furniture and goods for sale. The reader should refer to the description above of Chapman of Louth for a 9 bore fowler by Monck with a barrel signed Chapman.

Annotated directory of Lincolnshire gunsmiths

(Additional notes provided by D J Baker and the editor extend the listings into the 20th century)

Alford

John Blyth
South End 1849–68.

William Ginger
West End 1861.

Charles Edward Lewis
Gun and rifle maker, High Street 1900–13.

Charles Lewis
Church Street 1849; High Street 1861, (and bell hanger)

Joseph Lewis
High Street 1876–96

An advertisement for J Lewis in the *Alford Almanack and Diary*, 1883 is encyclopaedic!

J. Lewis, Gunsmith and Bellhanger, gas fitter and general ironmonger, High Street Alford, has in stock: Breech and muzzle-loading guns, rifles, revolvers and pistols. Ammunition of every description. Cartridges any kind and size. Gunpowder in canisters and in bulk, by any makers. Glass, bronzed, and gilt, chandeliers for gas and oil, petroleum, benzoline, and moderator lamps. All kinds of tin and copper goods made to order. Iron spouting of any pattern. Iron fencing. Iron bedsteads. Loose boilers, ovens and bottoms. Agent for any kind of kitchen range etc. Anglo American cooking and other stoves. Liquid manure pumps and Indian rubber hose pipe. Copper and iron furnace pans. Glass and globes of all kinds for oil and other lamps. A large quantity of petroleum, benzoline and other oil.

Charles Edward Lewis
High Street 1900–13.
Robert Mason
Market Place 1849.

Barton-on Humber
J. R. Rawson
High Street 1849.

Boston
James Bracebridge
27 High Street 1889; 22 West Street 1896.
Robert Chapman
Bridge Street 1826–35; West Street 1840–49 (latterly also a whitesmith and bellhanger).
J. Cole
On 20 August 1847 he advertised 'To journeymen gunmakers in the above line may meet with employment by applying to J Cole, 6 Bridge Street, Boston' and the next month ' J. Cole–newly invented breech plug', 24 September 1847.
David Dalby
1833
William Hen(s)man (late J. Trevitt q.v.)
19 Bridge Street 1905–19.
In 1909 'Practical gunmaker, locksmith, cutler, bell hanger, fishing tackle dealer. Cartridges and all sporting requisites and repairs a speciality.' An advertisement in several editions of Kelly's Post Office directory 'William Henman (late J. Trevitt), practical gunmaker, locksmith, cutler, bell hanger, fishing tackle dealer. Cartridges and all sporting requisites and repairs a speciality'.
John Hill
Wormgate 1842.
Henry Hurren
High Street 1849–56 (and cutler).
Eliza Hurren
High Street 1856 (probably the widow of Henry, deceased).
Peter Jackson
High Street 1893.
Luke Parkin
High Street 1826–42 (latterly also cutler).

Richard Quincey
   Bridge Street 1861.

Edwin Slingsby
   10 High Street 1861–76; 10 and 12 High Street 1882; High Street 1885–89

Probably related to the Slingsby whose workshop West took over at Retford after leaving Louth 1861–62. There was also a John Slingsby at Leeds and Pudsey in Yorkshire c.1840–65.

E. C. T. Slingsby
   10 High Street 1896–1900.

Slingsby Brothers
   10 High Street 1893–1935.

Herbert Thompson
   22 West Street 1900–05.

Joseph Towl
   Bridge Street 1835–61; 13 Bridge Street 1868.

Job Trevitt junior
   19 Bridge Street 1872–1900.

William Vauce (or Vaux)
   South Street 1826.

Richard Willows
   72 High Street 1882 (and ammunition dealer).

Brigg (otherwise Glanford Bridge)

George Henry Hockey
   Market Place 1892–1900.

Charles Leonard, gun and rifle maker
   12 Market Place 1926.

Lincolnshire Gun and Ammunition Co.
   11 Market Place 1930–35.

Frank W Lightwood
   12 Market Place 1909–22 (also Grimsby and Market Rasen).

J Lofley
   Market Place c.1843–61. There was a George Lofley at 45 Gallowtreegate, Leicester, 1862–64.

Mrs Maria Lofley
   Market Place 1868 (gunmaker and manufacturer of all kinds of breech-loading guns).

Lofley and Co.
   12 Market Place 1876–89.

Midland Gun Co. (dealers)
   12 Market Place 1905–09.
Joseph Parish
   1797
Richard W(h)ithers
   Butchery 1821.

Burgh-le-Marsh (Burgh in the Marsh)
John Parish Bartholomew 1876–92.

Caistor
William Brown
   1821
Mrs Ann Button
   Cornhill 1882 (ammunition dealer).
William Jolland Field
   Market Place 1834–61; Wooley Horse Market 1862.

Crowle
George Pheasant 1861
   High Street (Doncaster inserted in brackets) 1882–92.

Crowland
J Goodwin
   East Street 1868.

Gainsborough
John Cheatter
   Silver Street 1826; Bridge Street 1828–30.
George Hill
   24 Caskgate 1882.
Samuel Hudson
   Beast Market 1826.
Henry Jackson
   Queen Street 1840.
A Mr Jackson ,Gun maker, died 8 May 1849, (24 May 1849, *Eastern Counties Herald*).
Henry George Jackson
   Church Street 1841–44; Market Place 1849–68 (and bell hanger).
Jackson and Son
   39 Silver Street and Trentside 1919–22.

John Leadham

Beast Market 1826.

John Liversidge

Market Place 1840–44; Beast Market 1849; Market Street 1861 (see also Lincoln); Beast Market 1864.

The Lincoln, Rutland and *Stamford Mercury* 6 July 1838 has the following:

Market Place, Gainsbro'. J. Liversidge, gunmaker etc. is tendering his grateful acknowledgements to the gentlemen, sportsmen and inhabitants of Gainsbro' and its vicinity for the liberal and increasing support he has received since his commencement in business, respectfully announces that he has on hand double and single barrelled guns, pistols etc., warranted home-made and of the best material, which he is offering on the lowest terms with every other requisite for shooting.

J. L. begs to assure his friends that he will by punctuality in his engagements, moderation in his charges, and the best workmanship, endeavour to preserve the patronage which has been so liberally bestowed upon him. Old barrels re-bored on an improved principle and warranted to shoot close and strong NB. An apprentice wanted.

He was still at Market Place c.1842, at the Beast Market 1849 and Market Street 1861. A George Liversidge is recorded at 56 Steephill, Lincoln, in 1843 as running a shooting saloon (figure 41)

An advert of 19 June 1846 announces that Liversidge was 'in immediate want of a steady experienced workman'. On 20 August 1847 he was in 'immediate want of an experienced workman' and again on 28 January 1848 Liversidge advertises for 'an experienced workman ...(who) may meet with constant employment by applying to J Liversidge, gunmaker, Gainsbro'.'

His marriage to Eliza Morris, only daughter of William Morris of Walkeringham, school master, is announced in the *Hull Advertiser* 28 April 1848 and the *Eastern Counties Herald* of the 27 April. John Liversidge died at the age of 49 on 17 February 1849, announced in the *Hull Advertiser*, 25 February 1865.

figure 41: Number 56 Steephill, Lincoln, occupied by George Liversidge in 1843 as a shooting gallery; half way up the hill at junction with Danesgate.

Charles Frederick Liversidge

Market Place c.1867–72; Beast Market 1876; 29 Beast Market or 29 Market Street 1882–c. 1919.

C. F. Liversidge succeeded his father John Liversidge and an advertisement for 3 May 1867 records:

C. F. Liversidge, Gun Maker, Market Street, Gainsborough. Breech and

Muzzle Loading Guns, Rifles, Revolvers and Pistols of every description. Improved Patent Self-Loading Central Fire Breech Loading Guns. Rifles for Rook and Rabbit Shooting. Conversions and Repairs carefully executed. Implements of every description for the Sportsman and Rifleman. All kinds of Sporting Ammunition, Wholesale or Retail. Improved Leather Gun Cases. Dog Collars, Couples, Chains and Leaders.

He lived at 29 Market Place with his wife Annie, daughters Charlotte, Fanny, Louise, Florence and Grace, as well as three sons, Charles E, Arthur and Herbert. Louise is recorded as a shop assistant and Charles E as a gunmaker. He was one of the original members of the Gainsborough Volunteer Corps, initially a corporal but latter recorded as Battalion Armourer Sergeant Liversidge. A competitor at Bisley he won the St John Badge in 1890, the Lieutenants Prize in 1875 and 1896 and was the holder of ten cups including the Challenge Cup offered for the best shot in the 19th Lincs. Rifle Volunteers in 1866 and 1872. A prominent freemason he was secretary of the Yarborough Lodge for 36 years, lay office-holder at All Saints church and a staunch conservative. Liversidge was secretary to the Gainsborough Cattle Market Company and in December 1894 the prizes for the Gainsborough Fatstock Show were displayed in his shop window and he gave a handsome cruet stand for the best pig in the show. In September of 1894 he also showed stuffed specimens of seabirds (including gannet, guillemot, tern and black headed gull) shot by W. E. Marshall and R Walter Forrest on the Devonshire coast.

A postcard photograph posted in Gainsborough 1906 and signed Charles F Liversidge is addressed to H (for Herbert) Liversidge in Sydenham, London (figure 42). Bert as he called him was evidently C F's son. The card is a splendid view of the three storey shop the name LIVERSIDGE boldly painted between the uppermost and second storeys. A bowler-hatted figure standing in the doorway is probably Charles F Liversidge. The windows have adverts for Curtis and Harveys Smokeless Diamond and Amberite Cartridges and for Cricket, Fishing Tackle, Tennis Goods. Clearly visible in the left lower window is a row of guns in a rack and in the right hand window, tennis rackets, cricket bats and hockey sticks.

An undated advertisement tells us that the premises are three-storeyed:

figure 42: Premises of C F Liversidge, Market Place, Gainsborough, 1906.

with a large shop, where is kept in stock a large assortment of the most approved makes of breech-loading and other fowling pieces, breech and muzzle-loading rifles, revolvers and pistols, air and stick guns, breech loading cartridge cases, gunpowder, shot, caps, wadding, wire cartridges, flasks, pouches, bullets and bullet moulds, dram bottles, leather gun cases, cartridge carriers and bags and every requisite for the sportsman. Mr Liversidge also cleans and repairs every article connected with the gun trade or the wants of the sportsman. Fishing tackle by the most approved makers is always in stock; and Mr Liversidge devotes particular attention to all matters connected with lawn tennis, cricket and athletic requisites ... a good business is also done as engraver and bell hanger ...

Charles Liversidge died in April 1921 and he is described in the Gainsborough News as:

Outspoken almost to bluntness, a straight forward and honourable business man, Mr. Liversidge held the respect and hearty esteem of all who knew him and although he lived a decade beyond the 'allotted span' of life his death will be much regretted by those who knew him intimately.

An interesting reminiscence in the files of the Gainsborough and District Heritage Association was brought to the writer's attention by Mrs. D. Pearson who provided much of the biographical information. From c. 1897 the Liversidge establishment was described as a gunmakers and sports outfitters. Apparently one of the Liversidge daughters latterly sold women's clothes from the shop which was taken over by Cooper and Baumber for the sale of ladies and gentlemen's wear. Mr Baumber recalled:

... we moved from Lord Street, Gainsborough, to 29 Market Place in about 1927 [the directories indicate c.1917–18] ... there was a forge in the back of the shop for repairs and Mr Liversidge had a store off Pingle Hill for ammunition and guns. The shop had a cannon over the door and was called Cannon House, the cannon was eventually taken to Cleethorpes front gardens.

Presumably the latter was some sort of wooden or metal sign but no such item is visible in the photograph reproduced here. As recently as the 1950s the shop had received a communication from Spain offering guns for sale! A charming percussion pocket pistol, a box lock with turn-off barrel is signed LIVERSIDGE GAINSBRO (figure 43 and 44). Two identical box-lock, percussion pistols, not numbered as a pair, are preserved in Hull museums. Measuring 7¾ inches overall the 3 inch turn-off barrels have fluted exteriors (figure 45). The fluting is mirrored inside the muzzle for about a quarter of an inch but the barrels are themselves smooth of $7/16$ inch bore.

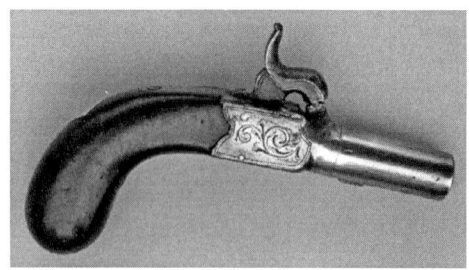
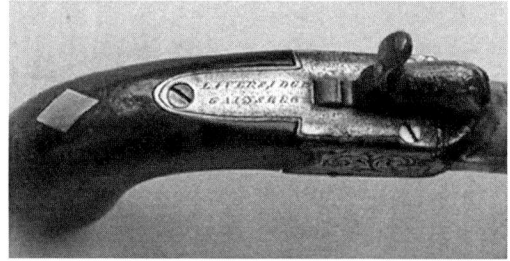

figures 43 & 44 (above left and right): Percussion pistol signed LIVERSIDGE GAINSBRO on top of the frame, on the tang behind the hammer.

figure 45 (right): Pair of percussion pistols signed LIVERSIDGE GAINSBRO on the tang behind the hammer (Hull Museum)

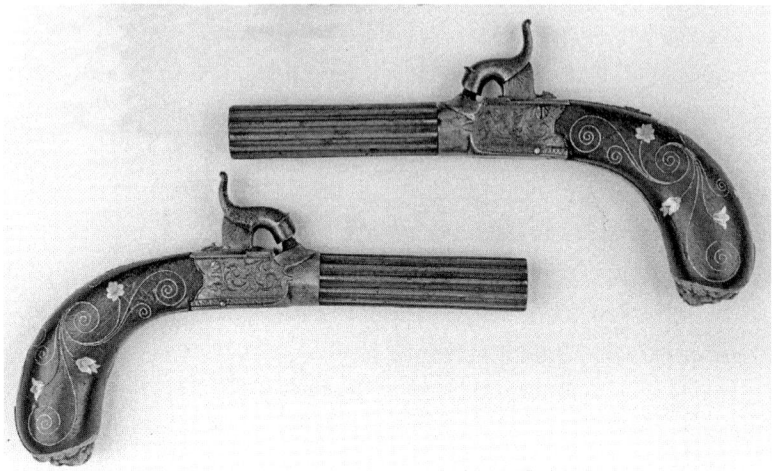

Each barrel is stamped with a Birmingham proof mark and a view mark on the underside of the breech. The butts, inlaid with wire tendrils terminating in leaves and flowers, have lion masks and oval escutcheons, all in German silver. The tang behind the hammer is engraved LIVERSIDGE, GAINSBRO'. An identical pair signed FIELD, OXFORD (William Field, Beer Street c.1841-44) is in the collection of the Whitby Museum, Pannett Park, N Yorks.

William Paris

Gunstock manufacturer 1810.

Charles Sherratt

Bulls Head Yard, Gt. Church Lane 1826.

Leonard Wiswould

Gt. Church Lane 1826-30.

He was in Birmingham, at Russell Street, described as a gun and pistol maker, c.1834-46. William Greener in The Gun (1853) recommends Wiswould's particular iron mixture, three quarters steel and a quarter iron, 'I never saw any iron with which I have been more pleased, both for its cleanness, and the beautiful way in which the steel and iron are mixed'. (pp 20-22). A 50 bore percussion box lock pistol, signed 'Leonard Wiswould Gainsboro', was offered along with a pistol by George Wallis of Hull as lot 268 in Bonham's 'Antique arms and armour' sale, 25 July 2007 (illustrated).

Grantham

George Dawson
High Street 1835; Market Place 1841; Westgate 1856.

George West Dawson
Westgate 1842; High Street 1849.

John Ed(g)son
Apprenticed to his father William; freedom in 1773.

William Ed(g)son
fl. 1765–80.

The Gun Shop
34 Westgate 1935.

John R Hanson
4 Westgate 1882–85 (see also Lincoln).

Bertie Beaumont Jenvey
20–21 Westgate 1913–26.

Jenvey and Tite
20–21 Watergate 1909.

Thomas Manton
Well Lane 1826; Castlegate 1830 (see notes under Stamford).

Joseph Manton
Castlegate 1830.

Edward Newton
fl. 1718–64 (died 1764) See note 1.

William Newton
From Nottingham, nephew of Edward Newton. Succeeded his uncle 1764 and died 1790 (see note 1).

Sports and Hardware Ltd, gun and rifle makers
34 Westgate 1930–33.

William Stovin
4 Westgate 1882–1905.

John Wilkins (John Willmer Burton Wilkins)
High Street, gunpowder preparer, c.1825–42 (probably son of John Wilkins, partner of William Newton, who succeeded to the latter's business in 1790).

Charles Willmer (established 1822)
Westgate 1822–76; 83 Westgate 1882.

Grimsby (Great Grimsby)

George B Abbott

232 Victoria Street 1935–36.

Frank W Lightwood, gun and rifle maker
122a Cleethorpes Road 1909–33; 3 West St. Mary's Gate 1919–22; 172 Cleethorpes Road 1935–87. See also Brigg and Market Rasen.

C. W. Lightwood is illustrated in the assemblage of photographs, portraits of the Gunmakers Association 1929.[60]

Ebenezer Lingard
150 Victoria Street 1872; 35 Victoria Street, West 1876–82; 154 Victoria Street 1885–93.

Ebenezer Lingard and Co.
154 Victoria Street 1892; 144 Victoria Street 1900–05 (see also Louth).

Thomas Lingard (son of Ebenezer)
Queen Street 1882.

Miles Roberts
Bull Ring 1840; Upper Spring Street 1856.

Holbeach

J Hardy 1856–68
High Street 1867.

John Blinkhorn Hardy
West Street 1876; High Street 1882.

John Charles Hardy
West Street 1885; West End 1889–1930.

John Rippin
Charles Street 1889–92; West End 1893.

Staunton Bros.
116 Corporation Street 1962–3.

Trent Guns and Cartridge Co.
Welholme Road 1935–6.

Trent Lead Pipe Co.
Welholme Road 1933.

Horncastle

William Shipley Brown and Co.
Bridge Street 1848 (and patent wadding manufacturer); 1856 (see also Spilsby).

In the *Lincoln, Rutland and Stamford Mercury* 15 September 1826:
Wm. S. Brown, Gun and Copper-Cap manufacturer, returns his sincere thanks to his friends and the public for their liberal favors, and begs to state to them that he has greatly reduced the prices of his Copper-Caps, as well as every other article, and at the request of several

sportsmen residing some distance from Horncastle, has appointed the following agents for the sale of them in the county; viz. Messrs Featherby and Sprague, Ironmongers, Lincoln; Mr Williams, Ironmonger, Sleaford; Mr Ashton, Ironmonger, Louth; and at the following prices:- Anti-corrosive Percussion Caps reduced from 20s to 14s per thousand; and the commoner kind, reduced from 15s to 10s per thousand.

From about 1841 the firm is known as William Shipley Brown and Co. On 30 October 1846 following the death of William Shipley Brown 'All persons having any claims, send particulars to his son Mr William Brown, gunmaker, Horncastle'. In 1849 the son is referred to as a patent wadding manufacturer and last recorded in 1856.

A two barrelled, percussion turn-over pocket pistol with brass frame and turn-off barrels signed BROWN & Co. on the breech tang is in the Scunthorpe Museum; 5¾ inches overall, 1⅜ inch barrel with ⁷⁄₁₆ bore.

Arthur Hill
Market Place 1905–35.

A Hill and Son
9 Market Place 1913–19.

B Tate
Millstone Street 1855.

Bryan Tate
Buttermarket 1849 (and bellhanger).

Richard Tate
Millstone Street 1856 (see description of Tate family above).

John Webster
Waterside 1856; Cagthorpe 1861.

Edwin Wilson (late Cartwright of Norwich; Rampant Horse Street, c.1841–83) Bridge Street 1861–8 (gun wadding manufacturer);16 High Street 1876–82; 5 St Lawrence Street 1885. At 13 Rampant Horse Street, Norwich, c.1886–c. 1905.

George Henry Wilson
9 Market Place 1889–1900.

Wilbraham
1797

Kirton-in-Lindsey
John Woffindin
Also bell hanger and whitesmith, 1848.

A 12 bore double-barrelled shotgun of c.1880–1900, signed Woffindin, is in the Baysgarth museum, Barton-on-Humber.

Lincoln

Richard Chester

1 Broadgate 1835; 23 Broadgate 1840-56.

The 1851 census records him aged 50 living at 14 Rosemary Lane with his wife and family. He is described as a gunmaker, born at Louth, and his wife Elizabeth and all their children were born at Lincoln, suggesting he learned his trade in Louth and moved to Lincoln soon after. Two of his sons Richard, 27, and John Henry, 19, are described as journeymen engineers.

Peter Clabrough

244 High Street c.1835-39.

A flintlock, box-lock, pocket pistol of possible Birmingham manufacture is signed CLABROUGH and LINCOLN on opposite sides of the lock; see fig.7, above. (County Museum, Lincoln)

Jane Clabrough

244 High Street 1839-46.

In an advertisement dated 13 September 1839 she refers to her deceased husband and in the *Lincoln, Rutland and Stamford Mercury* 5 June 1846 'Gun and Fishing Tackle warehouse, 244 High Street, Lincoln, Jane Clabrough respectfully informs her friends that she has engaged for the ensuing season a superior workman who has been employed by some of the principal gunmakers in London and the county which will enable her to execute in a satisfactory manner'. On 15 October 1847 she advertises Coles patent (breech plug?) and 18 August 1848 that Mrs Seels (late Clabrough) gunsmith is still at No. 244 High Street (to be eventually succeeded by J Hanson q.v.).

Jane Seels

244 High Street 1848-c. 1855; presumably Jane Clabrough after remarriage.

John Cook

63 Newland 1835-42.

Alfred Groom

13 Clasketgate 1922-33.

J Hanson

244 High Street c.1862-85; and executors of John Hanson 244 High Street 1885.

John Robert Hanson

244 High Street 1888. (see also Grantham)

Robert Hanson

244 High Street 1892.

L Hanson

1 Cornhill 1903-10 (and cycle maker).

Edward Lane

6 Silver Street 1849.

George Liversidge

56 Steephill 1843 (Shooting Saloon) (see figure 41).

This address is a substantial house half way up Steephill at the corner with Danesgate.

William Thomas

High Street, St Marks, 1835; 300 High Street 1840-43; 7 Strait 1849-50 (figure 46).

Wallis Bros.

364 High Street 1885-88; 156 High Street 1896; 156 High Street and 1 Cornhill 1899; 156 High Street and 4 Corporation Street 1900-05 (see also Spalding); 4 St Mary's Street (and cycle agents) 1907-22. See Sleaford entries for R, S. J. and W. R. Wallis)

Joe Wheater

367 High Street,1984-85; 3-9 Tentercroft Street 1986-98 (previously at 265 Anlaby Road, Hull; clay pigeon champion–British Open 1961, 1962, 1964, 1971 and 1972, Chatham Cup 1949, 1951, 1953, 1954, 1958, 1959 record six times, Olympic team 1956 Melbourne and 1960 Rome).

figure 46: Number 7, Strait, Lincoln (which links High Street and Steep Hill) occupied by William Thomas, 1843-1855.

Louth

Stanley R Arnold

27 and 29 Mercer Row 1926-33.

Day Bros.

35, 37 and 39 Mercer Row 1930-33.

H R Dimmock

27-29 Mercer Row 1935.

Edwin Dodson

Upgate 1841-42; Upgate 1849 (and dealer in fishing tackle); 1856.

Henry Dodson

Upgate 1861 (this is possibly an error for Edwin Dodson)

Edwin and Frederick George Dodson

14 Upgate 1868-92 (fishing tackle suppliers from 1872).

F. G. Dodson

14 Upgate 1892-96.

Jesse Parker Hodgson

figure 47: Upgate, Louth, 1970s; Lill's old shop on the left, in the midframe, and Lincolnshire Gun Co. on the near corner.

27 Mercer Row 1889–1909 (latterly 27 and 29 Mercer Row).

A. A. Hodgson
27 and 29 Mercer Row 1913–19.

Jonathan Kew
Market Place 1835; Mercer Row 1841–61.

Alfred Kew
27 Mercer Row 1868–85 (from 1872 fishing tackle supplier).

Michael Lill
Upgate 1826–35 (and whitesmith).

Lincolnshire Gun Co.
27 Upgate, Louth 1966–c. 1985; 6 Eastgate c.1986–88 (figure 47).

Ebenezer Lingard
26 Aswell Lane 1864–68 (see Grimsby). A 17 year old apprentice to George West in 1851; born at Fotherby 1834.

Michael Porter
Upgate c. 1828–31.
Born 1804 Michael Porter appears in the trade directories, 1828–31, at Upgate and in the 1851 census was staying at 125 Westgate with his mother. In the 1881 census he is described as unemployed (rather than retired) though aged 77! His birth place is given as South Elkington, a small village some three miles outside Louth.

Bryan Tate
Butcher Market 1826–35; Cornmarket 1841–42 (and whitesmith) (see also Horncastle).

Richard Tate
Butcher Market 1835; Cornmarket 1841–42 (see also Horncastle).
[There is also a David Tate, whitesmith, at Eastgate, 1842]

George West
Eastgate 1849–56 (and bell hanger); Fish Market 1861.

Joe Wheater (ex Lincoln and Hull) 'Wheater Fieldsports'
18 Eve Street 1999 etc.

Others
In the 1820 baptisms, St James, Louth, a Charles Phillips is christened, the son of Christopher William Sturman, gunsmith. George Smith, gunsmith, aged 20 appears in the 1841 census. A William Kime, 24, gunmaker, was resident at 56 Kidgate, Louth at the time of the 1851 census. In 1881, aged

54, and described as a gunmaker, he was living in Union Street with his family; his son Samuel aged 19, is listed as a coach body maker. Also in the 1851 census is William Badley, aged 31, Long Lane; born at Horncastle he is described as a publican, grocer and gun dealer. William Parker, gunsmith, living at 105 Westgate in 1851 was born at Barton-on-Humber.

Edwin Wilson, son of a baker, aged 20, 1 Mercer Row and John Croft, son of a tailor, aged 17, 43 Eastgate, are both described as gunmaker's apprentices in 1851.

A George Oliver is in the 1881 census at 40 Gospelgate, Louth, aged 17, he was born at Wykeham (presumably the village of that name in North Yorkshire) and the register of the Louth Burial Board records his death, aged 40, in Nottingham, buried 27 July 1903, in unconsecrated ground, implying he was a suicide. Also in the 1881 census George Whaley, 25, gunsmith, born at Lincoln, living at Trinity Lane, he was unmarried at the time.

In the 1950s the shop on the corner of Upgate and Mercer Row was occupied by the Lincolnshire Gun Co (figure 47).

Market Rasen

Walter H Coates
   2 and 3 Market Place 1919–33.

Frank W Lightwood
   14 Market Place 1909–22 (see also Grimsby and Brigg).

William Gifford Thomas
   King Street 1840.

John Woffindin
   Market Place 1882.

Sleaford

Samuel Bridges
   Westgate 1842–49.

David Clayton
   Old Sleaford 1835–41.

William Mouel Hooton
   South Street 1868–82; 43 Southgate 1885–1900; 15 Southgate 1905–35. He had been at Market Place, Wisbech, Cambs., in 1852.

John Jones
   Southgate 1849.

Orlando Keyworth
   Southgate 1848–50.

Edward Wakefield Lane
   Southgate 1840–42.

Spalding

Leonard Dalton
Hall Street 1821; Pinchbeck Street 1827–35.

Elderkin, established 1880; currently at 17 Broad Street and winner in 2003 of 'Best Gun shop' award, given by Shooting Times and Sporting Gun (figures 48 and 49).

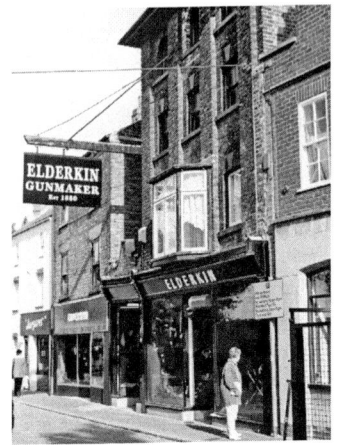 

figures 48 & 49 (above left & right): Elderkin; 17 Broad street, Spalding.

Charles Dickinson Jennings
Bridge Street 1868; 5 Bridge Street 1872; 5 Bridge Street, Winsover Road and Commercial Road 1876.

Samuel Roy Marrison
9 Cowbit Road 1885–93 (there was a Samuel Marrison in Norwich, Norfolk, 1821–53).

Joseph Tye
Bridge Foot 1848; Churchgate 1849–55 (and whitesmith); High Bridge House 1876; 1 and 2 Churchgate 1882.

Robert Wallis
Pinchbeck Street 1849–61 (locksmith and bell hanger).

R. Wallis and Son
Pinchbeck Street 1868; 17 Pinchbeck Street 1872.

Seth John Wallis
17 Pinchbeck 1876–82.

William R Wallis
44 Pinchbeck Street 1885–89.

Joseph Wright 1872
High Bridge House c. 1900.

Wright and Currey
1 Churchgate c. 1900.

Stamford

Thomas Bailey fl. 1821–35.

Thomas is recorded in the trade directories at Ironmonger Street c. 1821 and in the High Street c.1827–35. An advertisement in the *Lincoln, Rutland and Stamford Mercury* 12 August 1825 proclaimed

> High Street, Stamford. T. Bailey, gunmaker etc. grateful for the favors with which he has been honored by the nobility, gentry and others of Stamford and the neighbourhood, begs to return thanks for the same, and to assure his friends and the public in general that nothing shall be wanting on his part to merit future patronage. NB. Sole agents for Joyce's Anticorrosive Caps. To be sold, two excellent Pointers and a Setter, which have been shot to two seasons.

William Bailey

St John Street 1842–49 (probably the son of Thomas).

George Dawson

See Grantham

John Edgson

From Grantham, Red Lion Street 1790–1815

David Edgson 1810

Bernardo Gobbi

Ironmonger Street 1868–72

Thomas Manton (b.1750) fl. c. 1810–28

Manton was active in London c. 1810–20 and was in Grantham c. 1820–28, and also in Stamford in 1818:

> Thomas Manton (from Mr Jos. Mantons) gunmaker, St John Street, Stamford, respectfully acquaints sporting gentlemen and the public generally that he manufactures new and highly approved gun locks to prime with fulminating powder and which for the singular advantage of an instant and inevitable discharge even in the wettest weather is considered a desideratum in the sporting world. T.M. also manufactures locks upon the common principle of superior workmanship and everything else connected with his business in a style to which he confidently solicits public attention.
>
> (*Lincoln, Rutland and Stamford Mercury*, 20 May 1818)

Thomas was a first cousin of Joseph and John Manton. According to Bailey and Nie both Joseph and Thomas are recorded at Castle Gate, Grantham in 1827. Manton like Dawson (q.v.) may have had a presence both in Grantham and Stamford over several years. Joseph had suffered bankruptcy in 1826 and was not discharged until 1832.[61]

Thomas Monck senior
  Red Lion Square c. 1773-1825.
Thomas Monck junior
  High Street c. 1800-17; Red Lion Square 1817-24; Ironmonger Street 1825; Red Lion Square 1825; St John Street 1826-30.
Mary Monck 1830-c. 1832.
Thomas Bingham Monck
  St John Street c. 1832-c. 1856.
Edward Monck
  33 St Mary's Street 1861-92.
Richard Moore
  North Street 1840.
H. T. Starsmore and Co.
  33 St Mary Street 1905-09; 14 St Mary's Hill 1909.
J. Laidlaw Wood
  14 St Martins, High Street 1876-82; 33 St Mary's 1882-1906.

Wainfleet All Saints
William Hammond
  Market Place 1876-82.

Miscellanea
The 1885 Kelly's directory for Lincolnshire also includes entries for London based concerns:
  Charles Lancaster 151 New Bond Street and 2 Little Bruton Street, London W., inventor of the non-fouling, smooth oval bore for express and other rifles, also of four-barrel breech-loading guns, express rifles and pistols. Est. 1826.
  Gunpowder Manufacturers. Pigou Wilkes and Laurence Ltd. 11 Queen Street, London EC.

The key source of information other than trade directories is the *Lincoln, Rutland and Stamford Mercury* which also includes references to gunsmiths in neighbouring Cambridgeshire and Leicestershire e.g.:

Loughborough (Leicestershire)
Jesse Brown
  Baxtergate 1846; Mill Street 1862-64.
Thomas Bussey
  Ashby Road 1834-41(also Gallowtreegate, Leicester, 1846-49; Mrs. Ann do.1854).

Thomas Proudman
>High Street 1827.

18 June 1847 *L R and S Mercury*, 'Wanted an apprentice to an old established gun making business, apply personally or by letter, post paid, to John Sanders, gun and pistol maker, High Street, Loughborough.'

According to Bailey and Nie there was a John Sanders in Liverpool 1789-1860, and a Joseph Sanders in Leicester 1832-47 and also at Loughborough 1834-63. They found John Sanders listed for Loughborough only in 1848.

A Joseph Sanders also appears at Oakham, Rutland, 1856 and William Sanders at Oakham 1865. There was a William Sanders at Liverpool in 1803 and a Samuel Sanders, gun lock maker, Darlaston, Staffs. in 1854.

Melton Mowbray (Leicestershire)

John Marsh
>Market Place 1839-49

----Tyler 1849

T. Webster

5 August 1825 *L R and S Mercury*

>T Webster gun manufacturer etc Melton Mowbray, impressed with gratitude for past favours, begs leave to call the attention of gentlemen and sportsmen to his newly manufactured stock of percussion guns, on the most approved principles. Having a large stock of materials on hand before the advance took place he is enabled to offer the following low terms–A stub-twisted and patented double percussion gun at £8 8s; a single ditto same quality at £2 10s; and so in proportion. Old guns altered to percussion from 10s 6d each to any price. Copper caps and tubes on the lowest terms.

>T. W. in offering his superior sporting gunpowder, begs leave to return thanks for the distinguished patronage he has received, and to inform his friends that for cleanness, quickness of fire and peculiar strength it is not to be exceeded. Every other description of powder, shot etc. wholesale and retail on the lowest terms.

>NB. A second hand Forsyth and Co Double-Gun, nearly new, to be sold for £15, warranted to shoot well.

This may be the Thomas Webster who was at Edmund Street, Liverpool, in 1795.

Edward Whitehouse
>High Street 1854-c. 1870; Edward Whitehouse & Son to 1890; Edward Whitehouse & Co. to c. 1901; John Edward Whitehouse & Son, 11 High Street c. 1913; 9 High Street. In about 1917-18; Whitehouse & Son to c.

1932. Edward Whitehouse & Son opened a shop at High Street, Oakham (Rutland), c. 1874; John Edward Whitehouse c. 1883–97; Edward Whitehouse & Co. c.1928; Whitehouse & Son, c. 1930–c. 1940.

Wisbech (Cambridgeshire)

John Chapman
High Street 1829.

Robert Clarke
Old Market 1823–30.

Charles Culling
Little Church Street 1857–69.

Henry Foster
1845–69.

William Gamble 1821–24

17 March 1825, *L R* and *Stamford Mercury*

To Whitesmiths, Gunsmiths etc. To be let, with immediate possession, an eligible situation in the centre of the flourishing town of Wisbech, opposite the Market Place, comprising a good dwelling house, with show shop in front, and smith's shop adjoining the same, late in the occupation of Mr William Gamble, deceased, where the business of Whitesmith, Gunsmith and Bell-hanger, has been carried on for many years, in all its branches. The stock-in-trade, tools, shop, fixtures, etc. to be taken by appraisement, which will not exceed £300.

For particulars enquire (if by letter, post paid) of Mr William Dolby and Mr William Isley, of Wisbech, Cambridgeshire.

All persons having any demands upon the estate and effects of the late William Gamble, are desired to send in their accounts, and the persons indebted to the said William Gamble, are desired to pay the same immediately to the above Mr Dolby or Wisley, the executors.

This was evidently William Gamble senior who Bailey and Nie record at Market Place 1821–1824. Evidently his son was already in business and did not require any of the stock or tools, for he is listed, near New Inn, 1821–24 and in Union Street 1829.

William Mouel Hooton
Market Place 1852 (moved to Sleaford).

John Lewin Nixon
Upper Hill Street and New Inn Yard 1864–68.

Nottingham

Francis Britton
　36 Carleton Street 1846.

Samuel Brumitt
　Mount Street 1810–28.

Robert Dakin 1797

John Hetherington
　Bridlesmith Gate 1817–44.

John Hetherington Jnr.
　Bridlesmith Gate 1844–64.

John Hooke
　Lenton Street 1843.

John Low Jackson
　Low Pavement 1821–28 (patent no.4823, 29 July 1823, for a self-priming percussion lock; manufacturer to HRH Duke of Sussex).

Adam Jennard
　1797

John Micklewaite
　Listergate 1824.

Samuel Newton
　Bridlesmithgate, c. 1716–71.

Tom Wimsey also obtained copies of the wills of Samuel Newton, gunsmith, of Nottingham and his wife Elizabeth. Samuel was the brother of Edward Newton of Grantham and made his will 16 July 1733. In it he very usefully refers to the date of his 'marriage articles', 27 April 1716, and by the terms of his will devised his 'two messuages or tenements' in Bridlesmithgate, to his wife. One of these was occupied by him, the other by Catherine Trentham, widow. After the death of his wife their children were to benefit in equal shares i.e. William, John, Samuel, Jane, Ann, Elizabeth and Dorothy. The trustees were John Lowe of Derby, apothecary, his brother John Newton of Keisby (Lincs.), grazier, and his brother-in-law Samuel Oates (Oakes?), while Elizabeth was the executrix.

She made her own will 10 December 1766 when Samuel was clearly still alive since she leaves him the interest on £400 for his lifetime, 'the remaining part of the leggee my cossin Fferdinando Lowe left mee at me owne desposell'. After his death £150 was to go to their daughter Dorothy,[62] £20 to their son Samuel[63] (along with a gift of his note for £30 and any interest), £20 to their granddaughter Theadose (sic) Hesketh, £10 to another granddaughter Dorothy Hesketh and the residue to Dorothy Newton their daughter.

An affidavit from Thomas Tye, gentleman, of Nottingham and Rebecca Blaxsidge, widow, swore as to their knowledge of the deceased and that they recognised that the testament was written in her hand ; this document records that Elizabeth Newton died 1 March 1767. A bond issued 26 August 1771 sometime after the death of Edward Newton confirm that his will was duly administered in the absence of his deceased wife and executrix. Samuel probably died in early 1771 and certainly between December 1766 and that date. His brother Edward in his will dated 1 May 1764 gave Samuel £10 for mourning.

A boxlock, flintlock pistol by Samuel Newton, the slab-sided butt with silver wire inlay, is described in a recent article, along with images of the Newton premises in Bridlesmithgate. Mention is also made of a pair of high quality flintlock holster pistols,15 in. in length, sold at Sotheby's, London, 16 December 1975, lot 243 and also a pair of silver-mounted cannon barrelled pistols of 'Queen Anne' type, sold at Sotheby's, Sussex, 26 November 1996, lot 2,166. The butt caps in the form of grotesque masks have the mark of Jeconiah Ashley, active in London c.1737-65 . See Brian Godwin 'Samuel Newton, gunmaker of Nottingham' *Classic arms and militaria* XV, no.4, 2008, pp. 40-3.

John Oldbury
> Beck Lane 1846.

George Oliver
> Gunsmith, died aged 40 at Nottingham, see under Louth, above.

Robert Pattison
> Parliament Street 1834-42; Bunkers Hill 1843-64.

Newark (Nottinghamshire)

Newark burial registers on microfilm:

George Bailes
> Gunsmith, 2 January 1785.

A George Bailes was apprenticed 1738 and active in London until 1768-69, the son of William Bailes.

John Halland (Holland?)
> Gunsmith, 10 March 1796.

John Barker
> Gunsmith, 9 December 1798

Recorded on index cards in archive office:

PMSM 1/194 Invoice of Sam Cole of Newark 1663 1 gun 1 case pistols with holsters 1 sword 1 belt.

Other Newark gunsmiths encountered:

Isaac Barber

Born 14 September 1750 and died 26 February 1828 ; active on his own account 1773–1798; in partnership with Joseph Boaler, Market Pace, in 1804.

A pocket pistol , sold as lot 1091, sale 234, Wallis and Wallis of Lewes, 31 October/1 November 1977, illustrated pl.43; flintlock box lock, , 5 inches overall with a turn-off barrel 1½ inch, Tower proved, engraved 'Barber Newark' within oval. Sliding top thumb safety, throat-hole cock and concealed trigger; slab sided walnut butt.

Joseph Boaler

Market Place 1821–35.

Robert Boaler

Bargate 1829.

Joseph and Robert Boaler

Market Place 1840.

Boaler and Welch

Bargate 1827; Market Place 1831–42.

Thomas Doubleday

Boar lane 1821–32.

Edward Fisher

1796

Peter Flag

1796

Charles Johnson

Gunmaker and superintendent of Newark Fire Brigade, 22 Stodman Street; in partnership with David Nixon, Market Place, dissolved 1869.

Charles Johnson

Market Place 1869–72.

--- Nixon

1829.

Richard Killingley

1757

John Mason

1829–30.

David Nixon

Stodman Street 1829; Middlegate 1834.

Nixon and Lawton
    1870s.
Nixon and Smith
    1878.
Charles Smith and Sons
    Down to the present.
James Welch
    Kirkgate 1854–7.
John Welch
    1829–68.
Joseph Welch
    Kirkgate 1826–49.

Acknowledgements

A special thank you to Christine Wimsey, Tom's widow, who safeguarded his records until it was possible to prepare them for publication.

A big thank you also to Jean Howard, former curator of the Louth Museum (Louth Naturalists' Antiquarian and Literary Society); also to Ian Girdley, manager of the HSBC bank, Louth; P. Cadbury, Lincoln County Museum; Gareth Jenkins, Moyses Hall Museum; Bury St Edmunds; Malcolm Dolby, Bassetlaw Museum (Retford); Ruth Sutcliffe, Gainsborough Old Hall; Karen Waring, Gainsborough Library; Mrs Pearson of the Gainsborough and District Heritage Centre; Eleanor Nannestad, Community Librarian, Lincoln; Mark Rickards of the Stamford Museum; and to Gordon Bennett of Louth; all of whom shared information with Tom and myself or freely gave access to surviving firearms in their care. David Baker kindly provided photographs of a number of Lincoln and Gainsborough shotguns.

The archive offices at Lincoln and Nottingham also provided Tom Wimsey with copies of important documents and permission to publish their contents.

Appendix
The Nelthorpe Archive

Preparing the preceding material for publication I decided to investigate the deposit in the Lincoln archives made by the Nelthorpes of Scawby.[64] These documents reveal some interesting transactions with gunmakers in Lincolnshire and London, and also with the Wallis workshop in Hull. Surviving bills and receipts show that the successive baronets acquired their quality guns from London and relied on the local gunmakers for routine supplies of powder, shot etc and for work which is in the province of the whitesmith, like making keys. This picture may be a slight distortion since the series of vouchers is incomplete with sometimes whole years missing. It is difficult to believe that the Nelthorpes only used the Wallis workshop for mundane whitesmiths work.

The earliest receipted bill discovered for any gunmaker is one dated 29 June 1782 from John Manton,[65] which is early evidence of his activity since he had started on his own account only in the previous autumn. He was paid by Sir John Nelthorpe Bart (1744–99) a total of £7 18s 6d for:

> ...maintaining a Spanish Barrel in the best manner £6 16s 6d, Sliders to the bolts–6s 0d, Swivle (sic) and belt with buckle–5s 6s, Ram and Worm 3s 0d, Regulating a charger and shooting 2s 6d, punch for Hatt 5s 0d' (figure 50).[66]

It is likely Nelthorpe, probably best known as a patron of George Stubbs the artist, was aware of Manton's origins in Grantham and was thus persuaded to support this as yet youthful and untried gunsmith. Another receipt from Manton is dated 7 January 1787 when Sir John paid him £3 12s 0d for 'Fixing a pr. of double Barrels together, Browning etc. £2 2s 0d, Altering and repairing the locks, new mainspring, extra side nails etc £1 1s 0d, Ram and Worm, 100 flints 6s 0d'.[67] In neither case is a bill heading used or any indication given of Manton's address but we know that he was working in London, at Dover Street, from 1781 and that Sir John, the sixth baronet, had a house in Sackville Street, 1777–94 and subsequently leased Lord Sondes house in Berkeley Square. His successor Sir Henry Nelthorpe (1773–1830), the 7th baronet, lived in Red Lion Square in London.

figure 50: Bill of John Manton to Sir John Nelthorpe, 29 June1782, for mounting a Spanish barrel in the best manner etc.---£7.18.6. (Lincolnshire County Archive)

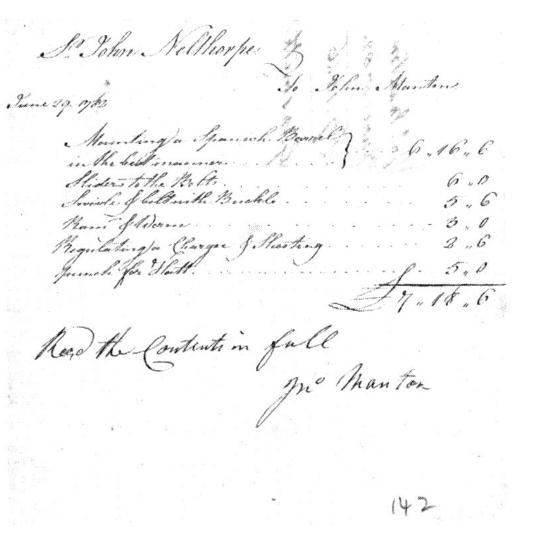

Sr. John Nelthorpe
To John Manton
June 29. 1782
Mounting a Spanish Barrel in the best manner ... 6.16.6
Sliders to the Bolts ... 6.0
Swivle & belt with Buckle ... 5.6
Ram & Worm ... 3.0
Regulating a Charger & Shooting ... 2.6
punch for Hatt ... 5.0
£7.18.6
Recd the Contents in full
Jno Manton
142

The next item is a bill with printed heading decorated with the arms of the Prince of Wales, from Durs Egg 'Gun Maker to their Royal Highnesses the Prince of Wales, Duke of York etc, corner of Coventry Street, Hay Market'. Dated 12 November 1789, again to Sir John, a total of £6 18s 0d was charged 'To a pair of best small pocket pistols double bolted locks secret triggers etc. £6 6s 0d. To a best flask for powder, ball, flints and key 12s 0d'.[68] Payment was made in Spring the following year, 1 April 1790.

On 17 April 1790 a bill amounting to £13 1s 0d was 'To a best steel mounted single gun, with gould (sic) pan and touch hole, silver escouchion and …?... for cipher £12 12s 0d, to altering and changing the case 6s 6d, to 3½ doz of best flints 2s 6d'.[69] A further bill from Egg, dated 3 November 1790 'To a new hammer for small pocket pistol and cleaning do 6s 6d, To cleaning a pair of double barrels taking the bruises out and a new head to ye ramrod with ferril 4s 0d, To a new ramrod with ferril and a stop on ye barr. 6s 6d'. A total of 17s 0d was paid 3 April 1791.[70]

The next account from Egg is dated 6 June 1795:

> To cleaning a double gun altering the locks and 2 new side nails 5s 6d, To a new ramrod with steel head and one to the other 7s 6d, To 200 best flints 13s 0d, To a new handle and hooks to the case and altering it and engraving the name on both the cases 9s 0d, To cleaning the pocket pistols, balls etc 3s 0d, To clean a best mahogany case for ditto 15s 0d'.

This bill for £2 13s 0d was settled on the spot.[71] On 12 November 1795, £4 6s 0d is the total 'To new stocking a single gun of the best with silver escutchions (sic) and oval £1 19s 0d, Paid carriage and porterage etc 3s 0d.' On the same account, on 22 January 1796, 'To cleaning a single gun and repairing the lock, a new cock, cock and jaw, a new hammer, hammer springs and nails, altering the springs etc done up the same as new £1 8s 6d. Paid carriage and porterage do 3s 6d'.[72] The final bill in the archive from Egg is dated 2 May 1796 at the top of the bill head and 2 January 1797 at the head of the list of items 'To a best new ramrod steel head 5s 0d, To cleaning and repairing a lock and a new sear spring 4s 0d. Carriage of do. 2s 6d'. Then on the same account, 4 July 'To 25lb of the best gunpowder £7 15s 0d [3s a lb.]'.[73] The bill was settled 5 July.

A small, entirely hand-written, receipt for F. S. Wooley : 'Rec'd June 7th 1793 of Sir John Nelthorpe Bart. Five pounds twelve shillings and seven pence, for goods etc as per bill' and added later '10s 6d for powder flask'.[74] Another tradesman, probably living locally near Scawby was J Dent who 25 September 1795 supplied Sir John with '2lb shott at 3d a lb.' and 7 November '4lb at 3d a lb.'

Another hand-written bill on a slip of rough paper is headed 'Hull Aprill ye 20 1794' and 'Sir Jno Nelthorpe to George Wallis. To foor duble garden kees £1. 0. 0 to one repard and tow desk keas 3s 6d, A razor sent by Mr Gale 3s 6d'.[75] The total of £1 7s 0d 'Recvd the contents George Wallis'. This is of course the noted Hull gunsmith and antiquary.

There is only one other bill for weaponry from the 18th century. This is from 'John Prosser (late Cullum) sword cutler and belt-maker to the King etc 9 Charing Cross', the royal arms splendidly engraved with lively supporters. Dated 8 March 1796 to Captain Henry Nelthorpe 'Sword £1 11s 6d, Kink (?) 10s 0d, Belt 10s 6d, Plate (?) 12s 0d, Gorget 12s 0d, Ribbons 1s 6d, Scarf (?) £2 12s 6d B ... and posting 3s 6d'[76], a total of £6 13s 6d.

There is a very long gap and then a hand-written receipt on plain, unheaded, notepaper to the 7th baronet, Sir Henry Nelthorpe (1773-1830), in '1824 To David Smith Gun Maker Janry 28 New silver sight to barrel 1s 6d, March 22 swivel tumbler to barrel 5s 0d, June 30 Gun lock repairing and cleaning 2s 0d, July 7 New Tumbler, screw etc 9d, Augt 10 New false breech and bolt etc to gun 7s 0d. Settled the above D Smith'.[77] A total of 16s 3d. A subsequent bill confirms that Smith is a local man 'Sir H Nelthorpe Bart. 1825 To D. Smith Scawby Brook March 200 Copper caps 3s 0d, April 26 100 ditto 1s 6d, August 31 300 ditto 4s 6d, Sept 13 150 copper caps 2s 3d, Sept 30 350 ditto 5s 3d, Oct 7 2 wash rods repairing 1s 6d, Nov 5 200 caps 3s 0d, Nov 9 spring to powder flask 1s 0d, Nov 26 Gun stocking and new rod, trigger plate bolt and screw guard altering, barrel scouring £1. 10. 0',[78] a total of £2 12s 0d.

Then, come a series of accounts from John Lofley of Brigg to the 8th and last baronet, Sir John Nelthorpe (1814-65) each of which covers the entire year January to December, for supplies of caps, shot, powder, spares, and repairs. The total for 1843 is £19 2s 0d and the headed notepaper is emblazoned with the royal arms though there is no explicit claim that Lofley had a royal warrant.[79] Lofley is a name found in Hull and district during the 19th century and he, in fact, tells us that he had come from the Wallis workshop in that town. The bill head bears the name of Goodwill and Lawson of Hull (engravers and printers)[80], and reads 'To John Lofley Gun Maker Market Place Brigg (from the late G Wallis, Hull) Manufacturer of the copper tubes and cap guns. Rifles, Pistols etc on the newest and most approved principle'. Similar bills for 1846 total £16 13s 6d,[81] 1850, £60 18s 3d[82] and an account for 1857 amounts to £44 4s 6d.[83] The latest bill from Lofley to Sir John that has been traced is for 1860 and totals £9 15s 0d; it was settled 17 January 1861 (figure 51).[84] In 1868 Mrs Lofley, presumably the gunmaker's widow, was listed in the trade directories and from c. 1876-89 the style is Lofley and Co. From c. 1905-09 the shop at 12

Market Place was occupied by the Midland Gun Co. A George Lofley was at 45 Gallow Tree Gate, Leicester, 1862-64; and 37½ Gallow Tree Gate c.1870-c.1878.

There are two bills to Sir John in the 1840s from the redoubtable William Bishop, 'the bishop of Bond street'. The splendid headed notepaper is emblazoned with the arms of Prince Albert and Bishop proclaims himself 'Agent to Westley Richards, gun manufacturer, by special appointment to his R. H. Prince Albert, 170 New Bond Street.

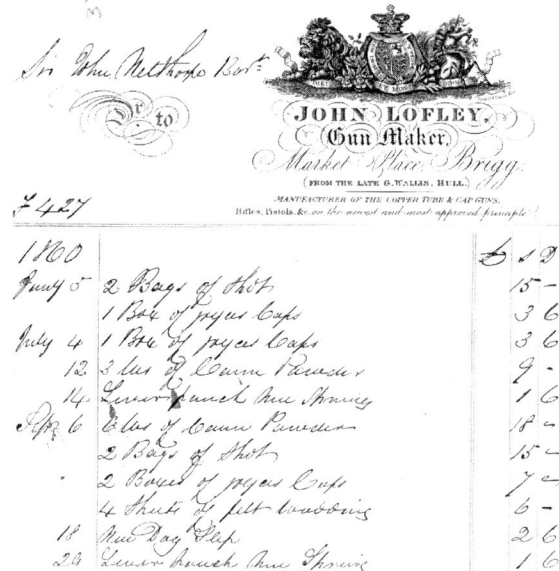

figure 51: Bill of John Lofley to Sir John Nelthorpe for 1860; settled 17 Jan. 1861 (Lincolnshire County Archive)

For ready money.' A bill headed 'Xmas 1844' to Sir John is evidently a reminder and the date below is 19 November 1836, 'To 2 boxes wadds, 18s loads rod 10s 6d Sling for do. 6s 6d. £1. 5. 0.'[85] Another bill dated 1847 to H Nelthorpe Esq. (Sir John's younger brother,1820-60) is also a reminder and below is the date 1843 'To examining, cleaning and browning double gun making locks go well and taking bruize (sic) out of barrels new fuze holes and cones £1. 10s. 0d 1000 caps 10s 1. Box wadding 8s. 18s 0d 1pr extra nipples 6s Shot pouch and strap 15s £1. 1s 0d Cash paid carriages of guns 1s 6d',[86] a total of £3 10s 6d. It is accompanied by a letter in which Bishop asks for payment of the bill 'owing to him a very considerable time'.

A bill dated 1 September 1846 from 'Wilkinson and Son Gun, Sword and Accoutrement Makers to Her Majesty etc' is directed on behalf of Henry Nelthorpe (9th Lancers) to H Grantham for payment. The sum of £12 13s 6d is for '1845 Dec 15 1 Regulation Infantry Sword £4 14s 6d 1 Gold Acorn and buff Sword Knot 12s 0d, Chamois And Macintosh cases 8s 0s, Rough case 3s 0d. 1846 Sep 1 1 Regulation Lt. Cavalry Sword £5 5s 0d, Crest and Cipher embossed 5s 0d, Gold and Crimson cord and acorn Sword Knot 18s 0d, Chamois and Macintosh cases 8s 0d'.[87]

The only other relevant bill is to Sir John Nelthorpe, dated 31 August 1859 from D. Philliskirk which, though referring to the hire of a saddle etc for 3s 0d, has a very interesting bill head. A decorative cartouche encloses the image of a sportsman aiming his gun while his horse waits patiently at a farm gate. It then reads 'D. Philliskirk Saddler and Harness Maker Filey Guns on the most approved principles to let Guns carefully cleaned. Dealer in superior powder, patent shot and every other article suitable for sportsmen. Cutlery of superior quality'.[88] This, like Lofley's bill head, was engraved by Goodwill and Lawson of Hull. David Philliskirk is in the trade directories c. 1840–58 at Queen Street, Filey. Since the 1820s this East Yorkshire fishing village has been a popular bathing place and seaside resort.

Notes

1. Tom Wimsey "Newton of Grantham" *Journal of the Arms and Society* vol. XVI, No.5, September 2000, p.292
2. Douglas Tate *Birmingham gunmakers* Long Beach, California 1997 pp 42-44
3. De Witt Bailey and D. A. Nie *English Gunmakers* London, 1978
4. Whiteface 'A British pneumatic airgun' *Guns Review* July 1981; 542-3.
5. David Baker and I. M. Crudgington *The British Shotgun* vol. I, London, 1979 esp. p. 120 which illustrates a Hanson patent shotgun. See also illustrated advertisement showing the patent shotgun in *White's* directory of Lincolnshire, 1872.
6. The premises still survive; a five bayed building with original central doorway inscribed Marchmont House, at the corner of High Street and Portland Street. It is now divided into two, a telephone shop and a Balti restaurant (pl.3).
7. Louth Wills, 53; apparently in Louth Town Hall.
8. Corporation records of Louth. (Louth Town Hall)
9. Wimsey , op. cit. p. 289.
10. Tom Wimsey 'Tate of Louth' *Guns Review*, vol. 24, No. 11, November 1984, p 747. Bryan Tate is listed in the trade directories at the Cornmarket in 1840. A daughter Mary was baptised 20 April 1801.
11. A David Tate was in business as gunsmith at Eastgate, Louth, in 1842.
12. He was succeeded by George Henry Tate and then William and Edward Tate, who both retired in the 1870s.
13. Wimsey,1984 op. cit. p 767 and in full colour as the cover along with a contemporary bill, described below. Present whereabouts of these items unknown.
14. Ibid. p 747.
15. H. L. Blackmore *A dictionary of London gunmakers* 1350-1850, Oxford, 1986.
16. Louth Wills, Lincoln County Record office: LCC 1844/220.
17. *Transactions of the Yorkshire Numismatic Society*, vol. 3, pt.1 (1927) pp.47-50.
18. A. G. Credland *Gunmakers countermarks on coinage; Journal of the Arms and Society* vol. XX, No.3, March 2011, p.93-101. These include a 2 reales silver coin, recorded in the U.S.A., stamped on the head 'Wallis/Hull'; George Wallis, father and son were active as gun makers in Hull c.1760-1833. Very neatly stamped the mark matches the poincon found on a silver-mounted (hall-marked 1804-5) target pistol by Wallis Jnr., in the Hull Museum. Not being an English coin it is less likely to have circulated and provided a means of advertisement. There is the intriguing possibility that it was intended as a 'ticket' for the Wallis museum of antique weapons and armour ; we know that Wallis Snr. introduced a charge of a shilling a head in 1794 so as to reduce the number of visitors who were interrupting his business.

19. Thomas Wilkinson Wallis *Autobiography of T.W. Wallis, sculptor in wood*, Louth, 1899, p 166 and A. G. Credland *Artists and Craftsmen of Hull and East Yorkshirer*, Hull, 2000, pp 112-126.
20. Dodson is listed in the *International Lexicon der Buchsenmachers*, from 1840-1863.
21. T. W. Wallis, op. cit. p 64.
22. See note 16. At a meeting of the Mechanics Institute in Louth, September 1871, Wallis is described as curator and a Mr Dodson was a member of the committee. Wallis had joined the Institute in 1867, see Wallis op. cit. p 70.
23. The print is advertised in the local newspaper, 14 May 1847, as just published, proof prints 5s and ordinary prints 2s 6d.
24. Dodson married a second time and in the 1881 census his wife is Sarah, aged 64, born at N. Ormsby. She died aged 73, 29 February 1890.
25. Cornelius Stovin *Journals of a Methodist farmer, 1871-1875*, London, 1982, p 25. Stovin was from Binbrook, Lincs., 10 miles north west of Louth.
26. A Merwyn Carey *English, Irish and Scottish firearms makers*,1954.
27. Louth and district diary in the *Grimsby Evening Telegraph* 2 November, 1983, p 6.
28. Obit. Louth and N. Lincolnshire Advertiser, Saturday 1 April 1899. Julia L. Dodson, widow of F. G. Dodson, died 13 May 1923.
29. Where his parents married 19 February 1821; Edward a widower to Mary Rhoads (sic), a spinster.
30. Two other daughters Anne and Susannah are listed, also Edward and Maximillian, the latter was the youngest, aged only four.
31. There was a considerable demand for the installation of wire operated bell systems in commercial premises and private houses, for summoning staff and servants and generally to keep in touch in large premises before the advent of the telephone and 'intercom'.
32. The 1861 census still has him at 60 Eastgate. There were four daughters and two sons; his eldest son George aged 14, gunmakers apprentice, and Frederick West, then only 5, also became an apprentice in due course. George West senior 38 was a widower by then, his wife Mary Ann West had died aged 36, 30 December 1859, which might have been a further incentive to move and make a fresh start.
33. Initially at Clumber Street, then at Carolgate in 1834 and Grove Street from 1843. Charles Slingsby was the principal immediately before the shop passed to West in 1861.
34. Apparently son of George Preston of Louth, at 66 Kidgate in the 1851 census, aged 30, and described as a powder compositor.
35. Youngest son of the second marriage.
36. George son of George and Mary Ann, baptised 15 June 1846 at Louth.
37. Newspaper cutting in the possession of (the late) Peter West. This lists the children of the second marriage Cecil M. West, Enfield; Jack West, Leicester; and Frank West, Retford; Miss Edith West, Leicester and Mrs Judy Ainger,

Leicester. The address of Cecil, apparently the eldest son is interesting and he may well have been on the staff of the Royal Small Arms Factory.
38. Nicholas son of George I, King of the Hellenes and Olga, daughter of Constantine, Grand Duke of Russia; born 1872 he married Helen the daughter of Vladimir, Grand Duke of Russia, and died in 1938. Father of the Duchess of Kent (Princess Maria); his youngest brother Andrew was father of Prince Philip, Duke of Edinburgh.
39. Original was in the possession of the late Peter M West. Frank West is presumably the Frank O. West who appears amongst the photographic portraits of the Gunmakers Association in 1929. See A. G. Credland 'Akrill of Beverley' *Royal Armouries Yearbook*, vol. 4, 1999, p 69.
40. Information from the late Peter M. West.
41. Col. Peter Hawker *Instructions to young sportsmen* London, 1833 (7th edition) pp 22-23.
42. Charles Lancaster became a very successful gunmaker.
43. In the 1844 edition of Hawker's *Instructions* there is an additional line "And he has lately brought out a new bench for rifling barrels" p 23.
44. Mary Godsall was at 1 Gloucester Terrace in 1872. Perhaps this name is not coincidental given his place of origin, Henry Godsall may well have invested some of his savings in property development.
45. Bailey and Nie op. cit.
46. Peter Hawkins *The price guide to antique guns and pistols*, 1973, p 93.
47. At the time of the 1851 census R. P. Hodgson was 32. A John Hodgson, blacksmith, New Market, is in the 1849 directory.
48. G. T. Teasdale-Buckell *Experts on guns and Shooting* 1900, see introduction p xxiii. Reprinted 1986.
49. Ibid.
50. Teasdale-Buckell, p. xxvii 'Hodgson has had a very varied experience, not the least interesting being that in which he taught the people of Japan to make guns on the English system'. *Louth Standard*, 27 January 1923.
51. An error for Luda, the latin name for Louth; the river Ludd runs through the town.
52. This is almost certainly the Robert Parker Hodgson who died 22 February 1908, the initial christian name having been omitted.
53. Or he had moved to a gunmaking business in Cambridge.
54. Douglas Tate *Birmingham gunmakers* Long Beach, California, 1997, p 5.
55. Wimsey 2000 op. cit.
56. Bailey and Nie op. cit.
57. Wimsey 2000 op. cit.
58. Bailey and Nie, op. cit.
59. A number of quotations from advertisements are given throughout the present text, not all are attributed to a particular source but in most cases it is safe to assume they are from the *Lincoln, Rutland and Stamford Mercury*.
60. A G Credland 'Akrill of Beverley' *Royal Armouries Yearbook* vol. 4 1999, p 69.

61. For a detailed exposition of the Manton family see W. Keith Neal and D. H. L. Back *The Mantons Gunmakers* London, 1967 and the *Manton Supplement* 1978; and D. H. L. Back *The Mantons, 1762-1828* Norwich 1993.
62. Dorothy was baptised 20 November 1730 at St Peters, Nottingham (Jane 9 August 1717, Ann 24 April 1720, Elizabeth 28 October 1724).
63. There were three children christened Samuel, 1 April 1719, 26 April 1727 and finally 4 May 1733; all at St Peters, Nottingham. William Newton was baptised 25 July 1722.
64. For background on the Nelthorpe family see guide to Scawby Hall, by Anthony Nelthorpe, 2008.
65. No address is given but at the time he was working at 6 Dover Street, Piccadilly.
66. NEL 9/4/142 Lincoln County Record Office. The punch is presumably a wad cutter to make wads from hat felt.
67. NEL 9/9/42
68. NEL 9/11/51
69. NEL 9/12/19
70. NEL 9/12/55
71. NEL 9/17/24
72. NEL 9/17/64
73. NEL 9/18/43
74. NEL 9/17/1
75. NEL 8/13/38
76. NEL 9/18/4
77. NEL 8/21/8
78. NEL 8/21/12
79. NEL 8/26/47
80. "Engravers, copperplate and letterpress printers and stationery"; they were at 4 Bowlalley Lane, Hull, in 1835 and c.1837-1863 at 22 Silver Street, close to William Needler's gunshop at 26 Silver Street.
81. NEL 8/29/345 Settled by H. Grantham Esq. for Sir John Nelthorpe Bt. 4 February 1847.
82. NEL 8/34/235 Settled 6 February 1851 by H. Grantham Esq.
83. NEL 8/37/29 Settled February 1858.
84. NEL 8/39/379.
85. NEL 8/2/30.
86. NEL 5/9/2.
87. NEL 6/9/26.
88. NEL 8/23/242.

References

Back D H L 1993 *The Mantons, 1762-1828*. Norwich.

Bailey De W & D A Nie 1978 *English Gunmakers*. London.

Baker D & I M Crudgington 1979 *The British Shotgun* vol. I, London.

Blackmore H L 1986 *A dictionary of London gunmakers* 1350-1850, Oxford.

Carey A M 1954 *English, Irish and Scottish firearms makers*.

Credland A G 1999 'Akrill of Beverley'. *Royal Armouries Yearbook* 4: 69.

Credland A G 2000 *Artists and Craftsmen of Hull and East Yorkshire*. Hull: 112-126.

Hawker P 1833 *Instructions to young sportsmen*. London, (7th edition): 22-23.

Hawkins P 1973 *The price guide to antique guns and pistols*. 93.

Neal W K & D H L Back 1978 *The Mantons Gunmakers*. London.

Neal W K & D H L Back 1978 *Manton Supplement*.

Stovin C 1982 *Journals of a Methodist farmer, 1871-1875*. London: 25.

Tate D 1997 *Birmingham gunmakers*. Long Beach, California: 42-44

Teasdale-Buckell G T 1986 *Experts on guns and Shooting*. 1900

Transactions of the Yorkshire Numismatic Society, vol. 3, pt.1 (1927) pp.47-50.

Wallis T W 1899 *Autobiography of T.W. Wallis, sculptor in wood*. Louth: 166

Whiteface 1981 'A British pneumatic airgun' *Guns Review*: 542-3.

Wimsey T 1984 'Tate of Louth' *Guns Review* 24, 11: 747.

Wimsey T 2000 'Newton of Grantham'. Journal of the Arms and Society XVI, No.5: 292